CoolBrandLeaders

AN INSIGHT INTO BRITAIN'S COOLEST BRANDS 2004

Australia • Brazil • Canada • Czech Republic • Denmark • Egypt • Finland • France • Germany • Hong Kong • Hungary • India • Indonesia • Ireland • Italy • Japan • Malaysia • Mexico • Morocco • The Netherlands • Norway • Philippines • Poland • Portugal • Saudi Arabia • Singapore • South Korea • Spain • Sweden • Taiwan • Thailand • United Arab Emirates • United Kingdom • United States

www.superbrands.org/uk

MANAGING EDITOR Angela Pumphrey

EDITOR Martin Croft

EDITORIAL ASSISTANT Emma Selwyn

DESIGNER Chris Harris

BRAND LIAISON DIRECTOR Annie Richardson

Special thanks to **Kristina Dryza** for conducting the initial research and **Mintel** for providing a considerable amount of market research material.

Other publications from Superbrands in the UK;
Superbrands 2004 ISBN: 0-9547510-0-0
Business Superbrands 2004 ISBN: 0-9541532-6-X

For Superbrands publications dedicated to: Australia , Brazil, Canada, Czech Republic, Denmark, Egypt, Finland, France, Germany, Hong Kong , Hungary, India, Indonesia Ireland, Italy, Japan, Malaysia, Mexico, Morocco, The Netherlands, Norway, Philippines, Poland, Portugal, Saudi Arabia, Singapore, South Korea, Spain, Sweden, Taiwan, Thailand, United Arab Emirates, United Kingdom and United States email: brands@superbrands.org or call 0207 267 8899.

To order a copy of Cool BrandLeaders 2004 please call 01825 723398

© 2004 Superbrands Ltd

Published by Superbrands Ltd
64 West Yard, Camden Lock Place, London. NW1 8AF

www.superbrands.org/uk

Printed in Italy ISBN: 0-9547510-1-9

What you will find on the following pages are examples of some great brands. They perform, delivering what they promise time after time. They do things differently. They connect and engage. To achieve Cool BrandLeader status is a tribute to creativity and flair certainly. It is particularly a tribute to acute observation of consumers, attention to detail and above all sheer hard grind year after year. However the brands on these pages have scaled further heights, being judged both cool and leaders. To win such an accolade, they must be finely in tune with the zeitgeist and have left their competitors some way behind. This suggests a rapport with individuals of an exceptional depth and relevance. As the voice for brands in the UK, the British Brands Group is keen to see an environment in which such brands can thrive, contributing to diversity, choice and a richer life.

JOHN NOBLE Director, British Brands Group

Most organisations crave enduring brands but in today's market being seen as 'cool' is the real accolade! Cool BrandLeaders celebrates those brands that make the grade. They possess almost magical qualities, becoming very desirable amongst style leaders and influencers.

Cool BrandLeaders brings together a great collection of case studies show-casing those brands, which convey an exceptional sense of taste and style. The many examples provide an insight into how to build that element of cool into your brands.

Of course getting there is one thing, staying cool takes a little bit more. It is noticeable however that many of the brands in this book change from year to year – testament to the importance of retaining your cool.

The Chartered Institute of Marketing is delighted to endorse Cool BrandLeaders, which continues to provide marketers with an appreciation of the discipline of branding and an insight into those organisations that epitomise those magical qualities – cool!

PAUL GOSTICK International Chairman, Chartered Institute of Marketing

Some brands reach the top the way New Yorkers do. Nakedly ambitious, they work late into the night, jockeying with competitors, never missing an opportunity to stab them in the back (though the front will do just as well).

Then there are mid-Western brands, who gain their success gradually but courteously through a combination of honest toil and good common sense.

The cool brands, meanwhile, live on the West Coast.

Apparently indifferent to the opinions of others, they just follow their own sweet path in life, leaving the office early to picnic on the beach. All their success has come without breaking into a sweat.

And you'd be amazed how much work goes into maintaining this pretence.

RORY SUTHERLAND Executive Creative Director, OgilvyOne Chairman, IPA Creative Forum

This is the third edition of Cool BrandLeaders and is part of a pioneering and exciting programme that was founded with the aim of paying tribute to the UK's coolest brands.

A dedicated Cool BrandLeaders Council (listed below) has been formulated consisting of eminent individuals who are well qualified to judge which are the nation's coolest brands. Each brand featured in this book has qualified to be featured based on the ranking of this council.

Through identifying these brands, and providing their case histories, the organisation hopes that people will gain a greater appreciation of the discipline of branding and a greater admiration for the brands themselves.

Beyond this cool branding bible, the Cool BrandLeader programme 2004 encompasses a dedicated Cool BrandLeaders website; Cool BrandLeaders Tribute Event in addition to other events about cool branding, as well as constant appearances by representatives of Superbrands on TV, radio and in newspapers commenting upon branding.

Cool BrandLeaders COUNCIL 2004

STEPHEN CHELIOTIS
Brand Liaison Director
Superbrands
Chair Cool BrandLeaders Council

RALPH ARDILL
Marketing & Strategic
Planning Director
Imagination

DANIEL BARTON
Head of Marketing
& Communications
Diesel Group UK

NICKI BIDDER
Editor in Chief
Dazed & Confused

FLEUR BRITTEN
Freelance Journalist

TONY CHAMBERS
Creative Director
Wallpaper*

SIOBHAN CURTIN
Marketing Manager
Piaggio

TRACY DARWEN
Managing Director
Naked Communications

TINA GAUDOIN
Style Director
The Times Magazine

NICOLA GREEN
Head of PR
O₂ UK

COZMO JENKS
Top British Milliner

MERITATEN MANCE
Director
Laundry Communications

MARY PORTAS
Founding Partner/
Creative Director
Yellow Door Creative Marketing

ALEX PROUD
Director
Proud Galleries

OWEN LEE & GARY
ROBINSON
Creative Partners
Farm

MARK RODEL
CEO
Ministry of Sound

ALON SHULMAN
Chairman
World Famous Group

DARREN THOMAS
Independent Marketing
Consultant

MATTHEW WILLIAMSON
Designer

CONTENTS

Foreword	9	Nokia	78
How does a brand remain cool?	10	O₂	80
Agent Provocateur	16	Orange	82
Asahi	18	PUMA	84
Audi	20	Richard James	86
Barbican	22	Rizla	88
BlackBerry®	24	Ruby & Millie	90
Bose	26	Saab	92
British Airways London Eye	28	sass & bide	94
Budweiser Budvar	30	Selfridges	96
Campari	32	Somerset House	98
Chanel	34	Sony Ericsson	100
Coca-Cola	36	Sophia Kokosalaki	102
Coutts	38	STA Travel	104
Dazed & Confused	40	Stella Artois	106
Denon	42	Stolichnaya	108
Dermalogica	44	Storm Model Management	110
Design Museum	46	TEAC	112
Diesel	48	The Lansdowne	114
Diet Coke	50	The Simpsons	116
Dust	52	The Sunday Times	118
GAGGIA	54	The Times	120
Goldsmiths College,		The Wapping Project	122
University of London	56	Tiger Beer	124
Guinness	58	Topshop	126
Hakkasan	60	Trailfinders	128
Havana Club	62	Vespa	130
innocent	64	Virgin Atlantic	132
Land Rover	66	V V Rouleaux	134
L'Artisan Parfumeur	68	Wallpaper*	136
Lavazza	70	Weber	138
Linn	72	Xbox	140
Malmaison	74	Directory	142
MTV	76		

ANGELA PUMPHERY
Managing Editor

The notion of cool almost takes you back to the playground. Who are the cool kids and how do you get into their gang? Why were you in their gang before the school holiday but not now? Or are you really effortlessly leading the pack with gay abandon?

It would seem that cool brands manage to tap into our psyche on an emotional level that we can't quite explain. In research for Cool BrandLeaders, Research International found that 80% of people become aware of a cool brand through word of mouth and that the qualities a cool brand should possess include originality, innovation and authenticity. However, it is interesting to note that 61% of those questioned think that cool brands can still be mainstream.

Those who create the right buzz and achieve Cool BrandLeader status face a difficult challenge not only to be recognised as such by style leaders in the first place, but to negotiate the increasingly fickle and demanding public. It's no secret that it is extremely difficult to be rated as cool and even more difficult to retain this lofty position. But like all experts, such brands make what they do look easy.

So, do some brands just emanate cool through every pore or is it more a question of monitoring every move with a continually developing strategy? Well, the jury is still out on that one, but such is the alluring attraction of Cool BrandLeaders. The stories of those who have made it are diverse and come from a wide variety of markets, but they all have that special something. Read on and some of the mysteries of cool will be unravelled…

STEPHEN CHELIOTIS
Brand Liaison Director
Superbrands
Chair Cool BrandLeaders
Council

RALPH ARDILL
Marketing & Strategic
Planning Director
Imagination

Cool is often about the journey not the destination. A journey of discovery between the brand and the consumer that forges a genuine bond of ownership and loyalty – 'I've found this and it's mine.'

Those of us that embrace cool are happy to invest our time and energy in the pursuit of cutting-edge trends, products, services and experiences yet it is often the 'discovery moments' themselves that become essential in creating the sense of mystique, desirability and authenticity we have for the brands that remain cool.

For cool brands it's often a game of hide and we will seek...

DANIEL BARTON
Head of Marketing &
Communications
Diesel Group UK

A brand should not worry about whether it is cool or not, but should instead nurture brand character. Not worrying is after all one of the defining characteristics of cool.

Otherwise, the secret isn't formulaic, but rather something that should be innate. If a brand wasn't cool and then suddenly achieved that status through some fortunate shift in trend or accidental association or even (heaven forbid) a clever agency, then when that situation changes, so does the image of the brand.

If we must define what a brand should do to try to remain cool, it should employ its target market (ensuring the company mindset and tone of voice is the same as its consumers), break the rules where possible and innovate in all areas.

Above all, it is the apparent effortlessness of a cool brand that will be the ultimate protector of its status. So like I said, don't try too hard.

NICKI BIDDER
Editor in Chief
Dazed & Confused

A cool brand has to have integrity and authenticity. The product or service it is selling needs to deliver on every level: quality, design and originality. Cool only works if it's a by-product, a side effect of delivering on all of the above rather than the end goal.

Staying credible has got to be about staying true to the distinctive personality and values that mark it out as different in the first place. This takes confidence. Consumers need to feel that confidence and the passion of the people behind the brand for the product they create: cool is an expression of affirmation not cynicism. The ultimate and most important affirmation of all comes from the community of personalities that make a connection with the brand and adopt it, not only bringing their brand to life, but also, if it's relevant, keeping it cool in the process.

FLEUR BRITTEN
Freelance Journalist

TONY CHAMBERS
Creative Director
Wallpaper*

SIOBHAN CURTIN
Marketing Manager
Piaggio

Trends that live fast die young. Nothing kills the concept of cool faster than overexposure and the epidemic adoption of a trend. Take Burberry and its ubiquitous checks – now so commonplace (and ripped off), the brand has been accused of being an emblem of the oik.

Prada, a brand that has preserved its pole position over the last decade, limits production of key pieces. Waiting lists for its trophy bags are quickly closed to maintain the cachet of owning one – it is simple 'treat them mean, keep them keen' psychology. If you missed out on this season's bag, the chances are you'll be in line ever earlier for next season's. Miuccia Prada restricts further publicity by very rarely granting interviews.

To remain cool, a brand needs to evolve its image and product continuously to stay ahead of the game. As soon as a concept is considered cool by the general public, it is time to move on.

In a fickle, superficial, short attention span world, holding on to something such as the 'cool factor' can be an enormous challenge. Try too hard and you'll reek of desperation, sit on your laurels and next time you look up you'll discover you've been left behind. The only way to succeed is to constantly evolve without ever losing sight of your DNA. Good design lasts forever, so if you have that to start with you've a strong foundation to build on.

The catwalk mentality must never be adhered to from a brand perspective: respect fashion but don't fall victim to it. A brand can remain cool even if it slips in and out of fashion. If you believe in what you do, stick to what you do, but never become complacent. Sometimes it's cool to be uncool for a while.

A brand that has been deemed cool has to work particularly hard at maintaining its appeal, preventing consumers moving onto 'the next big thing'. It needs to be able to evolve and develop but it must retain its core values and stay true to its personality.

The very notion of what is 'cool' changes from person to person. To maintain attraction, you need to know your brand and your audience very well, as having a clear direction and identity will always be cool. It is a question of consistently regenerating, rather than occasionally innovating.

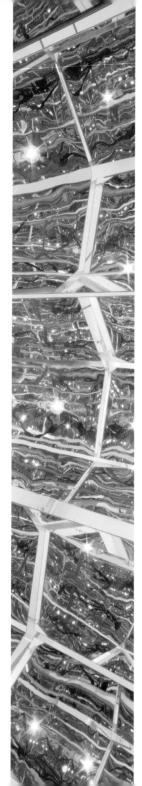

TRACY DARWEN
Managing Director
Naked Communications

Not giving a fuck about what others think because being cool is about being attitudinally distinctive, having immense self-belief, knowing your own mind, and doing your own thing. We can all recognise it, some of us can define it, even fewer have it but, importantly, none of us can achieve it. Those who think it is a destination will struggle to stay there. Only the cool know that it is about a sense of being. It is not something to work at, you've either got it or you haven't. If you are still reading this it is fair to assume that you haven't.

TINA GAUDOIN
Style Director
The Times Magazine

There's an irony in the fact that by the time that most of us get round to thinking that something or someone is cool, they or it no longer is. It is the very process of becoming 'cool' – wittingly or unwittingly that creates the buzz. The moment, for example, that you see a different watch (think Bell&Ross) or a new pair of jeans (this week it's Yanuk) and an impulse tells you it's a 'must have', you are potentially participating in the creation of cool. To qualify as 'cool' (and 'cool' is a pretty nebulous term) a product should be Exclusive, Elusive or Evolving. A product doesn't need to be new to be cool. In the case of individuals such as Alistair Cooke or Marilyn Monroe breathing is not necessarily a pre-requisite either. Critical mass is generally a cool killer. There are exceptions – the new Mini, David Beckham, Jaffa Cakes and Birkenstocks; but these things have transcended cool, they are icons.

NICOLA GREEN
Head of PR
O₂ UK

Brands which think they are cool, rarely are. Brands which say they are cool, most certainly are not.

An honest understanding of what consumers actually think is the first step towards ensuring the maintenance of a credible cool brand. The arbiter of cool is the consumer, not the marketer. Cool brands surround themselves and have a dialogue with credible influencers and media, whose 'cool status' is inherent and un-contrived. They work with them as partners, accept their counsel and do not try and impose false rules.

To remain credible demands constant brand evolution – of both content and direction. In this way, consumers and media alike will always have a fresh and interesting experience. Cool brands always stay ahead – on the cusp of the zeitgeist, not lagging behind and continually re-invent themselves – but always remaining aligned to the cultural undercurrents that truly guide society.

COZMO JENKS
Top British Milliner

MERITATEN MANCE
Director
Laundry Communications

MARY PORTAS
Founding Partner/
Creative Director
Yellow Door Creative Marketing

Coolness is highly intangible and hard to qualify but a brand remains cool because of a number of things.

A brand's identity needs to be timeless yet have the ability to change with the times and remain topical. Not following the fashion but leading and making it. Appeal must be broad and have an element of aspiration.

Brands often use the power of association to retain their cool, employing certain celebrities, models, countries, cities and a variety of other tools to reaffirm and demonstrate the brand's values. There is always an element of risk with this method as there is a reliance on the association which the brand cannot completely control. This tactic can be a sure and fast way of securing the elusive cool factor when done right.

The best brands remain cool by just being themselves and not trying to be anything else.

Truly 'cool brands' are cool because they have a unique and individual character to begin with. A brand is able to maintain it's cool by understanding the balance between reality and publicity, keeping it's prestige and not becoming complacent in the face of the mainstream. It's about keeping it real, and associating with people and events where there is a clear relationship and not just sticking a logo on anything that pays.

The world of brands is in an exciting and energising state of flux.

Every label, designer, retailer – high street or luxury is now tuned into branding.

They all know how to play the 'branding' game and some very well and very cleverly.

But what truly makes a brand cool?

No matter what clever marketing, aspirational imagery or campaigns are dreamt up to promote brands the only way that true coolness is achieved is through simple product truths. And how you tell them.

It's no longer about pretending to be something you're not.

The brands that remain cool are the ones that the consumers want because they connect emotionally with them and they deliver the promise.

And that means that they don't have to try too hard. Cos as we know trying too hard is just so deeply uncool….

ALEX PROUD
Director
Proud Galleries

OWEN LEE & GARY ROBINSON
Creative Partners
Farm

MARK RODEL
CEO
Ministry of Sound

How does a brand remain cool? By evolving in time to maintain credibility; i.e. changing your image or product ahead of the game. A brand has to remain innovative, daring and one step ahead to remain cool.

The best brands know this means that some projects will miss the mark or flop and that some will have very understated or subtle results, but this element of risk is at the core of what it is to be cool. Lastly the brand also has to focus on impressing the opinion former.

Topshop is a good example of a brand achieving both these goals by using this high risk seemingly low reward policy: whether it be by staging a burlesque fashion show in an east end boxing ring, snaring the latest models for their campaigns or hiring illustrator Daisy de Villeneuve, the immediate results are difficult to measure but long term rewards have proven to be huge.

Cool is a slut that's best ignored. It will sleep with a beer, a fashion brand, a magazine, even a coffee machine. And drop any of them on a whim. Chase it and you're sure to lose it. It's better just to keep on making great cars, desirable clothes or whatever it was that first attracted cool to you. Become obsessed with cool, and it'll dump you and move on.

If one were to apply science and mathematics to the 'How does a brand remain cool?' question the answer is quite simple. As follows;

$$r/jy=1/(3*sqrt(2*pi()))*exp(-0.5*pow((x-5)/3,2))=cool$$

Easy! So there's the answer – now all brands can apply the solution and be cool forever. Not.

The fact is no scientist ever worked it out and no scientist ever ran a brand.

And indeed, if one were able to answer the conundrum, the brand in question would no longer be 'cool'.

So just keep using instinct, focus, stay true to what you do and all I can guarantee is no brand was ever 100% cool 100% of the time. In fact, doing some uncool things is actually the best test of any brands metal. Until you've fucked-up and emerged from the other side still alive you can't gauge yourself on the coolometer anyway.

So the real measure of whether a brand is cool is if you've been forgiven for those moments when you're weren't.

ALON SHULMAN
Chairman
World Famous Group

DARREN THOMAS
Independent Marketing
Consultant

MATTHEW WILLIAMSON
Designer

Controlled Answer: I think it is very rare for a brand to remain cool indefinitely. A brand can still remain credible and relevant but it is inevitable that a time will come when the brand is 'cool' no longer. This is for the simple reason that the definition of cool changes and is affected by a huge range of influences while a brand in the strict sense of the word has to remain loyal to its brand values and brand identity. A brands cool credentials are firmly established when the brand goes beyond being part of a current trend and becomes part of a (perceived) cool and desirable lifestyle.

Cynical Answer:
Any way it can!

Never stand still to preen and congratulate yourself, never stop and think that the job is done – or you'll soon lose it. Keep moving by creating and innovating, you need to continue the momentum. Keep surprising, challenging, entertaining, being different, and keep producing great ideas and great products. If you manage that whilst remaining true to what your brand stands for, you build anticipation within your consumers, maintain relevance, and nurture an emotionally engaging relationship that will have them dying to see and hear what you're going to do next. How cool is that?

A brand remains cool by keeping up to date with its customers – nothing remains static so no brand is intrinsically cool – it takes hard work and a cool head!

Agent Provocateur

Agent Provocateur, more than any other company, has championed the 'lingerie as outerwear' revolution. It spawned the explosion of lingerie into the fashion world and is the only truly credible lingerie brand on the fashion map.

Joseph Corre and Serena Rees opened the first Agent Provocateur shop in London in 1994, and the media frenzy it caused has not yet died down. The pair's vision is still very much to create high quality designer lingerie that stimulates, enchants and arouses both wearers and their partners. As Corre and Rees say, "A woman wearing a scrumptious pair of turquoise tulle knickers promotes in herself a sexy superhero feeling which exudes itself as a confident and positive sexuality."

Agent Provocateur contemptuously dismisses the very British, very prudish attitude that anything to do with sex must be sleazy or smutty. Corre and Rees wanted to be provocative, to rattle the cage, but also to offer something colourful, very beautiful and very fashionable – and, most importantly, to show that sensuality and sexuality are nothing to be ashamed of.

The service the brand offers is a very intimate one, and underlines its belief that the way a garment feels is just as important as how it looks. Rather than a mass experience, it offers an intensely private, wholly personal one, where the focus is on the individual and the garment, the environment and the service.

Shunning meaningless mass advertising, Agent Provocateur's shop windows, cinema advertising, catalogues and events communicate with customers and admirers in a more intimate way. The boutiques especially

are emporiums decorated in a boudoir style which complements the erotic and sensuous lingerie on display.

Corre and Rees say, "Our visual world is translated through everything we do, our photographic campaigns, our interiors, our employees. We believe they should reflect our product. They should be glamorous, intimate, comfortable, and fashionable, justify your fantasy and have a sense of humour."

Agent Provocateur has also expanded beyond lingerie, designing and producing complementary accessories such as shoes and jewellery, and recently ventured into the world of music. In early 2004, it launched 'Peep Show', an album showcasing fourteen eclectic tracks unfolding a journey of sexual discovery, encapsulating the intimacy and erotic personality of the brand. Although the influence Agent Provocateur has had on high fashion has filtered down to the high street this position has been strengthened by the diffusion range, Salon Rose sold exclusively in the UK through Marks & Spencer.

Agent Provocateur also has a highly successful fragrance and beauty line, with Agent Provocateur Eau de Parfum winning best new female fragrance at the Fifi awards. The signature fragrance complements a host of beauty products from scented candles through to a luxurious body range.

As Agent Provocateur enters its tenth year, it remains committed to creativity, led always by the instinctive understanding of that which is beautiful and, of course, of that which is erotic. In addition to its UK boutiques Agent Provocateur has successfully opened stores in New York and LA. With its continuing expansion and opening of further stores within North America and other strategic worldwide locations. Agent Provocateur is set to continue taking lingerie out of the bedroom.

agentprovocateur.com

Asahi
ASAHI BEER

> **Super clean, super crisp, super dry & Super Fly**

Japan has a well-deserved reputation for producing high-quality, stylish products – and Asahi, one of Japan's oldest premium lagers, is no exception. Asahi Breweries was established 115 years ago, and is currently the biggest brewery in Japan. The core brand, Asahi Super Dry has also travelled well and is now the world's seventh biggest beer brand (Source: Impact 2002).

The name Asahi, pronounced 'a-sa-hee', means 'Rising Sun', and the brand is the beer of choice for a young, urban, stylish, socially active crowd, who appreciate its clean, crisp flavour with a hint of citrus and contemporary, slightly elitist image.

honed to perfection

PURE BEER: JAPAN STYLE
www.asahibeer.co.uk

Not content with launching Japan's first canned beer way back in 1958, in the late 1980s Asahi Breweries began to study the changes that were taking place in Japanese food culture – by understanding what people ate, it hoped to create the finest-tasting beverages to complement those foods.

The result was Asahi Super Dry, launched in Japan in 1987 and in the rest of the world soon after. In the UK, Asahi profited from the popularity of imported premium beers and sales of Asahi Super Dry have increased steadily since its introduction, particularly in London.

The brand has been brewed in Prague since 2000, and in order to ensure that the Asahi sold in Europe is as fresh as that in its native Japan, Asahi naturally ensures that it is made to the same stringent specification as it is in Japan. Ingredients include the finest quality water, malt, maize, hops and rice.

Over the years, Asahi has won many industry awards and accolades, more recently the 1999 and 2000 Award of Excellence for Advanced Business Facilities and the Second Grand Prize for Ozone Layer Preservation, both from the Nihon Keizai Shimbun, and the Minister of Environment Award from the Japan Industrial Journal.

In line with the current warmth towards Japanese style, which envelops the bar and restaurant sector, trendier establishments all over the country have been recognising Asahi. It can be found in urban cool bars, clubs, hotels and restaurants including Alphabet, Lab, Zuma, Nobu and Taman gang, along with more traditional Japanese venues.

Asahi, keen to be seen at the best launches and parties, has sponsored some of the UK's most famous young artists, such as Tracy Emin, Sarah Lucas, Gavin Turk and Damien Hirst, whose White Cube gallery show in Hoxton saw more than 1,000 people swigging Asahi on a balmy evening…

The brand is a major supporter of London Fashion Week, appearing at events such as Fashion East and Eye to Eye, and has been involved with a host of other big bashes – the infamous Return to New York parties, collaborations with the clubnight Shindig in Newcastle, the annual DJ Top 100 party at Turnmills in London, parties to celebrate the success of the Sony Playstation, the launch of football and fashion magazine Paper, the re-launch of the Barbican galleries…
The list goes on.

Asahi also supports cult films: most recently, it teamed up with Buena Vista Home Entertainment to celebrate the release of Quentin Tarantino's Kill Bill Volume 1 on DVD and video.

Asahi's advertising continues to go from strength to strength. Simple, strong visuals which draw on the brand's Japanese heritage emphasise the premium nature of the product and the quality of its ingredients, and appear as poster ads on the London Underground and press ads in style magazines such as GQ, Metro Life, the Leeds Guide and Manchester's City Life, while branded rickshaws also wind their way through the crowded streets of central London – all carefully targeted to reach the brand's urban and cosmopolitan potential followers.

seek inner purity

PURE BEER:JAPAN STYLE
www.asahibeer.co.uk

asahibeer.co.uk

AUDI

Audi has become the byword for intelligent, sophisticated, German technology. But it's also about an emotional response to progress, not just technology for technology's sake.

August Horch, a pioneering engineer with a reputation for being able to solve complex problems, set up his first company in 1899. By 1901 he had created his first automobile and the following year he began using lightweight alloys to reduce mass – this same principal is still in use today in the latest manifestation of the A8, where the body is around 50% lighter than if it were made of steel.

In 1909 Horch, whose surname means listen in German, started a new company, Audi, from the Latin for listen. His cars won a string of races, a tradition that continues to this day. Audi dominated British Touring Cars with the A4 in the 1990s and won the Le Mans 24 Hour Race in 2000, 2001 and 2002.

In the 1980s, its advertising slogan Vorsprung durch Technik entered the English language and even made its way into the song Parklife by Blur. It is still in use today as it sums up not only Audi's technical excellence but also its emotional attitude to design.

> Advanced technology, sophistication and head turning elegance, tempered by pure emotion

The news for 2004 is the new Audi A6, the first model range featuring Audi's new face – a grille that will feature on all models in the future. A trapezoidal shape incorporating the existing front grille, number plate housing and extending down to the front bumper, it gives the car an aggressive, sporty stance, and echoes the race cars of the 1930s.

The A6 is a sports saloon with low-slung windows and coupe-like roof line, and is targeted at the extremely competitive executive segment. This car takes on some of the innovations seen in the A8: MMI allows central control of all the car's functions; DVD navigation,

radio, CD, TV, telephone, radio traffic messages and set up of the car are all operated with one hand, using one knob and four function keys.

Radar based adaptive cruise control keeps the car a pre-selected distance from the one in front, automatically controlling speed, which helps on long journeys or in bumper-to-bumper traffic.

The bendy headlights – officially known as dynamic adaptive headlights – follow the course of the road ahead as a function of steering angle and road speed and so help you see round corners.

The multitronic® gears combine the sporting benefits of a manual gearbox with the convenience of automatic transmission, featuring stepless or continuously variable transmission.

The quattro® permanent all wheel drive is unique in its marketplace, driving power to whichever wheel can best use it, while lights, windscreen wipers and even brakes will automatically respond to wet weather.

The media spend on the A6's launch is the biggest and most comprehensive ever undertaken by Audi in the UK, with a spectacular TV ad featuring optical illusions that challenge the car to adapt to any driving conditions. Post-production on the ad was by Framestore CFC, the company behind the internationally acclaimed Walking with Dinosaurs TV series. Print and outdoor executions feature the car made from the words Vorsprung durch Technik, showing it to be at the core of the model.

Audi also appeals to the emotions with its other marques – the unmistakeable Audi TT, the Audi S4 quattro and the Audi A8, a luxury saloon with Audi advanced technology and the spirit of a sports car.

And as part of the company's commitment to design it has set up the Audi Design Foundation which has so far awarded over half a million pounds to young designers to help them bring their ideas to life.

audi.co.uk

barbican

PHOTOGRAPHY BY MIKHAIL BARYSHNIKOV

How fickle are fashion and fortune – yesterday's ugly ducklings are today's handsome princes. The much reviled Barbican 'pile' is now a listed building and admired by architects for its monumental strength and integrity.

Designed in the 1960s and constructed in the 1970s, the Barbican Centre was opened in 1982 by Her Majesty the Queen. Owned, funded and managed by the Corporation of London, the third largest sponsor of the arts in the UK, it is open 363 days a year and presents a diverse programme of world-class performing and visual arts, encompassing all forms of classical and contemporary music, international theatre and dance, visual arts and design, and a cinema programme which blends first-run films with special themed seasons.

In the last few years, millions of pounds have been spent on refurbishing, redeveloping and renewing the arts centre, so that while the exterior may be pure late 20th century modernism, what goes on inside is pure 21st century in its marriage of classical and contemporary.

The Barbican programme of performances was once the sole preserve of Shakespeare and traditional classical concerts. Today, it is the epitome of cool. Indeed, the whole complex is vibrant with contemporary creativity: new art shows, commissioned multi media work, unexpected artistic fusions – a constant cross-fertilisation of a wide range of different arts, catalysed with energy, yet never ignoring the building's classical roots.

Names from all corners of the globe fill the programme diary. Within just one month recently you would have seen Russell Maliphant rubbing shoulders with Bernard Haitink, while Grayson Perry opens a new gallery, Robert Wilson rehearses Black Rider with Marianne Faithfull, children's animation enlivens the cinema, Batsheva dances from Israel and Canadian puppets sit alongside Valery Gergiev's Prokofiev cycle.

Excellence, innovation and the best in international collaboration are now accepted as normal for the Barbican. But it is also a centre for the best of the traditional arts, too, with the London Symphony Orchestra and the Vienna Philharmonic Orchestra as stern benchmarks of quality. There is a rigorous approach to contextualising all of the different artistic work the Barbican offers a home to, with open access workshops for schools, families and others interested in learning more.

Such a huge range of diverse artistic forms and expression could be bewildering for the average punter, and certainly has been in the past. Only three years ago, for example, the Barbican included within it a myriad of excellent but unresolved mini brands, each perfect in its own right, but none of them working together to express any overall brand identity.

By contrast, in 2004, the centre's growing confidence as an international leader in the performing and visual arts and the growing homogeneity of its approach to programming – with the inclusion of multiple art forms, but driven by an increasingly singular aesthetic – has allowed the Barbican to recreate its own identity, and through it speak more clearly to its audiences, both old and new, with a singular brand voice that represents core values of leading, international, quality and excellence.

The Barbican's team is proud to lead public taste and to create tomorrow's arts agenda. Its audiences seem keen to follow. And today's artists want their work to be seen there. The Barbican now stands for all that is best in the arts – excitement, exploration, entertainment and delivery, in a format and a setting that is increasingly setting the standards for other arts centres to follow across the world.

Arts centres were once thought to be dinosaur institutions: the Barbican proves this wrong. Far from being at risk of extinction, its time has now come.

PHOTOGRAPHY BY WOYZECK AFTER GEORGE BÜCHNER, BETTY NANSEN THEATRE, BITE:02

PHOTOGRAPHY BY JANINE JANSEN

barbican.org.uk

BLACKBERRY

Imagine

Discover
BlackBerry

www.blackberry.com/europe

Go. Your world goes with you

BlackBerry® is about the freedom of being in control. Someone with BlackBerry can go where they like, when they like, and still manage their communications, information, business and life. They don't have to make choices just so that they can be near their information. They will always be able to take the call, read or respond to the email, plan the diary and read the presentation.

Research In Motion (RIM), the company behind BlackBerry, a market and technology leader in wireless communications, was founded in Waterloo, Ontario, in 1984 by Mike Lazaridis, inventor, entrepreneur and philanthropist and still RIM's co-CEO and President. Today, RIM has over 2,000 employees and offices in North America, Europe and Asia-Pacific.

In 1999, Mike Lazaridis came up with the idea of 'pushing' email to a device that could fit into a pocket – BlackBerry. Five years later, BlackBerry has well over one million users worldwide, with more every day.

BlackBerry is about success. It is for people who have information and business relationships to manage and decisions to make. It is about energy – immediate access to information and communications, alert to what they need and when they need it.

Most of all, BlackBerry is about partnership. BlackBerry is a tool and an ally – a pocket-sized resource that can be depended

Explore

on to keep the user in touch with work and the other things that matter. Quietly and unobtrusively, everything they need is there. Easy to use, dependable, indispensable.

The international award-winning BlackBerry is a solution that comprises software, services and advanced BlackBerry wireless handhelds with integrated email, phone, SMS, browser and organiser functionality.

BlackBerry exists in versions for corporate and individual use. Business and personal email is pushed directly to the handheld wherever and whenever – no effort required. Research conducted in 2003 suggests that users gain nearly an hour a day by being able to manage their email on the move.

BlackBerry is more than just a product. It is an experience. Once someone has tried it, it's very difficult to live without. Over 90% of customers who trial BlackBerry go on to buy.

BlackBerry users include everyone from employees in multinational law firms, global banks and government organisations to Hollywood film stars, musicians and international athletes.

Leading network operators across the world are working closely with RIM to introduce BlackBerry to corporate and professional customers. In Europe these partners include mmO2, Orange, SFR, TIM, Telefonica, T-Mobile and Vodafone.

The BlackBerry experience will soon be available on other handsets as well. Partners include Nokia, Sony Ericsson, Samsung, HTC and Siemens and software platforms PalmSource, Windows Mobile, Symbian and other Java devices.

Recognition for RIM's technology and innovation include an Emmy and an Oscar.

BlackBerry has become a cultural phenomenon, featuring in pop videos, fashion photo shoots and cartoons. Why? Because it works. It doesn't ask someone to do anything that they don't already do – it just lets them do it quicker and more conveniently. From looking up addresses in their corporate address list to making calls and filing e-mails, BlackBerry is completely intuitive.

BlackBerry. Cool because it changes forever the way we do things.

blackberry.com

Discover BlackBerry

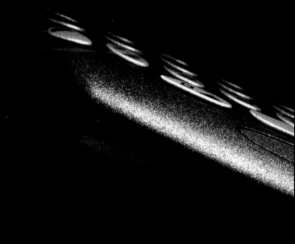

www.blackberry.com/europe

BOSE®
Better sound through research®

Better sound through research®

Bose believes that audio products exist to provide the highest quality music for everyone, everywhere – that music, not equipment, is the ultimate benefit.

In order to deliver on this promise, Bose combines high technology with simplicity and small size, so its home entertainment systems sound superb, while remaining easy to use and accessible to all.

Bose Corporation can look back on a 40 year history of making top-quality equipment. The company was founded in 1964 by Dr Amar G Bose, then professor of electrical engineering at the world-famous Massachusetts Institute of Technology. In the 1950s, he began researching psychoacoustics, investigating the relationship between reproduced sound as perceived by people and the same sound measured by electronic instruments, so developing and patenting advanced audio technologies.

MIT encouraged Dr Bose to start his own company and create products based on his patents, which he did with great success. Today, Dr Bose is still chairman and technical director of Bose Corporation, now a US$1.6 billion company. All of the profits are reinvested in growth and development, which explains why Bose loudspeakers are the best selling speaker brand in the US and throughout the world.

Bose sets the standard for high performance audio in the home, products which combine award winning patented technologies with advanced ergonomic design to deliver high performance sound, elegantly and simply. Top of the range Lifestyle® systems offer a huge range expandability – you can play four different audio sources independently and simultaneously.

Bose is also renowned for its superb Jewel cube speakers, the latest generation of Bose Direct/Reflecting® speaker technology. Similar in size to a mobile phone, they deliver crystal-clear midrange and high frequencies for music and film, so you get rich, room-filling surround sound from elegant tiny speakers that complement the interior. As with all Bose products, what you don't see is the technology that makes it work.

The ADAPTiQ® audio calibration system is another technological breakthrough from Bose, and one which ensures people get the very best performance from their home entertainment systems. Every room where you

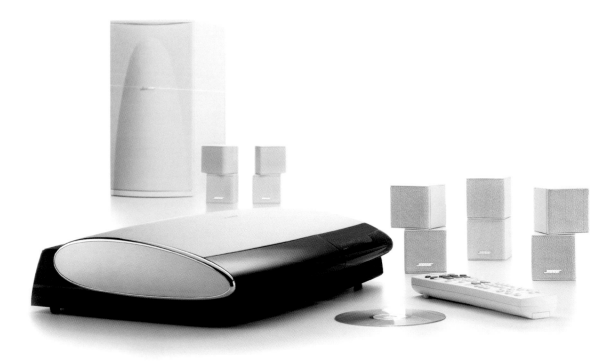

watch movies or listen to music is different. And every variation – from room size and shape, to window locations and floor coverings – can affect the audio quality of even the most sophisticated surround sound and music systems.

In line with the Lifestyle® system philosophy of offering superior performance coupled with greater ease and simplicity, the ADAPTiQ® audio calibration analyses the acoustics of your living space and automatically adjusts your Lifestyle® system to that particular room, so you get the most from the music system. Move your Lifestyle® system to another room, and you can just use ADAPTiQ® all over again to find the best possible set-up.

Although Bose is best known for its high-end speakers and home entertainment lifestyle systems, other product ranges include Acoustic Noise Cancelling headphones (bought by consumers who want no interference with their enjoyment of their favourite music, and pilots who cannot afford to be distracted by stray sounds), the Wave® radio products and in-car music systems.

If you go into any stylish bar, restaurant or hotel in the UK – or the world for that matter – you are likely to find that Bose speakers have been installed, while the company's products have appeared in advertising campaigns for Levi's, AOL and many other famous brands. Numerous films and TV shows have used them, including 'Love Actually', 'Friends' and 'Absolutely Fabulous', while Jeremy Clarkson recently covered their Quiet Comfort 2 headphones on BBC2's 'Inventions That Changed The World'.

Bose – using world-class technology to deliver world-class sound.

bose.co.uk

BRITISH AIRWAYS
London eye

The British Airways London Eye has quickly become one of Britain's most famous landmarks. It instils quiet pride and passion in its citizens and awe and amazement in all visitors. As well as providing spectacular views it also animates the skyline, gives a whole new perspective on the city and has helped to inject new life into London's South Bank.

But it almost didn't get off the drawing board. The Eye was designed on the kitchen table of London architects David Marks and Julia Barfield as an entry for a competition to create a structure to celebrate the Millennium.

The competition was eventually abandoned but Marks and Barfield knew they had a project worth pursuing – the biggest observation wheel in the world. With favourable coverage from the London Evening Standard and support from the public, the plans reached the attention of British Airways who decided to form a partnership with the architects and provide the loans to get the project started.

> **British architecture, innovation and engineering at its inspiring and visionary best**

The ingredients of the wheel are simple – a universal desire to see the earth and cities from a great height and the natural human fascination with scale, daring structure fused with beauty.

It's also a tremendous feat of engineering. Experts from across Europe were involved in its manufacture and the population of an entire Alpine village tested and re-tested the embarkation process on a mocked up boarding platform.

Shipping the various components to London was a complicated business and delivery had to be carefully timed with the tides so that the largest parts could get under the city's bridges safely. Southwark Bridge was the tightest squeeze, with clearance of only 40cm.

In a short time, the London Eye has become a symbol of modern Britain and is now the capital's number one visitor attraction. It has won a large number of architecture, design, tourism and people's choice awards and part of its success has been the careful positioning, design and management of the brand.

The London Eye is a superb venue for parties, events, product launches and even weddings, with couples tying the knot 135 metres above the capital. Packages such as the champagne capsule – with its priority check in and fast track boarding – remain hugely popular with consumers and corporate customers alike.

To keep the experience ever fresh, the London Eye team has introduced a number of joint tickets with a variety of top attractions, galleries and restaurants. These joint tickets encourage repeat visits and offer customers the very best of London through one easy booking. For example, the London Eye River Cruise Experience, which was launched in August 2002, has been extremely successful. The 40 minute circular cruise has commentary in English, French, German, Spanish and Japanese and highlights include the Houses of Parliament, the Tower of London and St Paul's Cathedral.

Whatever motivation leads visitors to the London Eye – whether it is to celebrate a special occasion, to see London as they've never seen it before, or for the sheer thrill of travelling 135m in the sky – they keep on coming. Perhaps it's because it's a remarkable piece of engineering, and an outstanding landmark; perhaps it's simply because of its graceful beauty.

ba-londoneye.com

See London
up here

enjoy a meal
down here

Combine a flight on the London Eye with a meal at a great restaurant, all from as little as £24.50

For more information about this and other offers call **0870 5000 600** or visit **ba-londoneye.com**

Conceived and designed by Marks Barfield Architects

BRITISH AIRWAYS
London eye

Budweiser Budvar®

An iconic brand, craft beer and classic lager

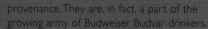

Budweiser Budvar is an idiosyncratic brand which has the unique distinction of being both craft beer and international classic, very much in tune with a younger generation of drinkers wary of the claims of big brewing and the blandness that globalisation process inevitably brings.

They are prepared to pay that bit extra for the best and are concerned about what they drink and eat, what is in it, where it comes from and whether it has real – as opposed to invented – provenance. They are, in fact, a part of the growing army of Budweiser Budvar drinkers.

In one sense, Budweiser Budvar has an aristocratic pedigree, with 700 years of uninterrupted brewing history in its home city of Ceske Budejovice in Southern Bohemia. In another sense, Budweiser Budvar is a youthful brand that thrives by keeping its promises.

In the UK, it is the number one Czech imported premium lager; overall, it is the number three imported premium lager and the number six most drunk premium imported lager. In 2004, it enjoyed year-on-year growth in sales volumes of 46%, in a sector which declined by 5%.

Youthful it may be, but the brand has wide appeal. It is the lager preferred by cask ale drinkers and the beer of choice for wine buffs. This is due in no small part to its craft beer status.

Being a craft beer means being brewed according to traditions laid down by generations of brew masters, not number crunchers, and never under licence but only at source. During the 100 day brewing cycle (90 days of it lagering), only natural products are used — whole hops (and they have to be female and virgin), malt made from wheat from the Hana region of the Czech Republic (home of all the great lager barleys) and water from the brewery's own underground ice-age lake, together with the brewery's own strain of yeast.

The brewing recipe has hardly changed since 1896 and Budweiser Budvar has always said it has no intention of doing so now for the sake of a quick buck or short term commercial advantage.

The other aspect of the brand that endears is that it is the only all-Czech owned brand that still flourishes on an international scale, the other once great beers now being in the hands of big brewing. This, plus the much publicised and on-going trademark dispute with the world's biggest brewer, have helped to make it iconic. It was not for nothing that Budweiser Budvar sponsored the Anglo-Czech film Dark Blue World, a story of Czech spitfire pilots during the Battle of Britain.

Czech it may be, but the brand has managed to enter into the mainstream of British life without losing any of its Central European mystique. A recent ACNielsen survey of the UK's top 200 alcoholic drinks brands found that Budweiser Budvar had moved up from 81st place in 2002 to 71st place in 2003.

A regular sponsor of events like the Edinburgh Festival and of events featuring young talent in the arts, music and theatre, the brand makes itself felt in local activities and is the only lager recognised by CAMRA.

Budweiser Budvar, the product of one relatively small Czech provincial brewery, has always been true to its roots; and, as a result, it became — and still is — one of the world's greatest and best loved beers.

budweiserbudvar.co.uk

CAMPARI

Red Passion — glamour, fascination, tension, transgression and class, Italian style.

Passion — red passion to be precise — is the true essence of Campari. The world of Campari is intense, filled with multi-sensual emotions. A world of desire, sensuality and eroticism. A world of red.

Gaspare Campari first invented the Campari formula in 1860, and in 1882 it was taken over by his son Davide Campari, who in turn started what is today the sixth largest player in the international beverage sector – the Campari Group.

The Campari recipe has remained unchanged since 1860: the ingredients used are the same now as they were then. Campari is 100% natural, made from herbs, plants and fruit, infused in water and alcohol. Campari can be enjoyed in many different ways: on the rocks, as a cocktail (Campari is the vital ingredient of classics such as Negroni and Americano), or as a long drink. Campari must always be served chilled to enhance its balanced flavour.

Drinkers of Campari are described as dynamic, modern, active, spontaneous and sociable. They are refined and don't settle for the ordinary or the banal. They defy convention and are not afraid to express their own individual needs.

Campari is cool, erotic, glamorous and at the same time passionate. Whatever Campari does is done with enthusiasm and true commitment. Campari is never half-hearted or detached. There is a tension that is inherent to the brand; but this tension is good, because it makes Campari one of a kind.

RED PASSION

Brand extensions of Campari include CampariSoda and Campari Mixx; these brand extensions are aimed at different target markets. CampariSoda is a single dose mixture of Campari and soda water, and was first developed and launched in 1932, in a bottle designed by famous Italian artist Fortunato Depero, one of the founders of the Futurist movement. This bottle has remained unchanged since then, and has become a design classic, used by interior designers and artists to create exclusive pieces of furniture such as the 'Campari Light' designed by Ingo Mauer. Campari Mixx is a Ready-to-Drink extension of the brand, first launched onto the Italian market in 2002 with a range of refreshing flavours. It won the Italian 'Packaging Oscar' for Design and Communication in 2003.

Campari's distinctive communication began at the beginning of the 20th century, through graphic posters and press advertising created by famous artists such as Leonetto Cappiello, Adolfo Hohenstein, Enrico Sacchetti and, of course, Depero. In 2004, Campari's innovative attitude towards advertising and marketing can be seen from the partnership between Campari and MTV. 'MTV Recommends' showcases the hippest artists around Europe and is sponsored exclusively by Campari.

The shape of the Campari bottle is simple elegance – ageless and always fashionable. Although the glass and label have had several revamps throughout the years, the bottle has always kept its timeless personality.

Campari is vibrant, edgy, erotic, sensuous and passionate. Campari is glamorous, stylish, fashionable, temperamental, active and fascinating – a state of mind and an expression of individual style.

Campari truly has no direct competitor. There is no spirit quite like it anywhere in the world – not in taste, image or history and it is for this reason that Campari is in a class of its own.

CHANEL

Fashion passes. Style remains.

Chanel's philosophy of design is simple, practical and comfortable, yet always elegant – and, at its heart, rebellious. And that has been true for nearly 100 years, since Gabrielle Chanel – known to all as Coco – began making hats and then dresses.

Coco Chanel's ambition was to liberate women from the tyranny of conventional, early 20th century dress, all corsets, wide-brimmed hats, stiff skirts and heavy chignons. She believed luxury was as spiritual a need as love – but luxury, for her, was always low-key and stylish, never brash and vulgar.

She hated being called a genius, and would rather be remembered as a craftswoman and as the champion of understatement. For her, what you don't see was as important as what you do – "luxury is when the inside is as beautiful as the outside" – and would rip apart seams or reset shoulders at the last minute before a show. She even lay on the floor so she could check that hems were perfect.

She looked outside the conventional for inspiration, and freely borrowed from men's clothing, creating that clear, masculine cut which, worn by a woman, imparts an air of fragile elegance. During World War I, she overcame a shortage of dress fabrics by using jersey – until then only used for men's underwear – to create stunning, sleek clothes. Later, she would introduce women to tweed, again giving it her own inimitable twist.

Her creativity was not restricted to clothing, either: she took existing ideas of what jewellery was for – ostentatious show during the evening – and reinvented them. Her jewellery was designed to be worn throughout the day, to enhance a woman's beauty and sense of self, not to demonstrate vulgar wealth.

And then there are Chanel perfumes, toiletries and cosmetics. Today's enormous range of beauty products all refer back to the original Chanel No. 5 perfume. Created for Coco by the legendary parfumeur Ernest Beaux in 1921, No. 5 was epoch making: a complete break with the past's heavy, mono-floral scents, it recaptured the simplicity of the soap Coco used as a child. Paradoxically, it is an incredibly complex formulation, with more than 80 ingredients – "a construction of the mind," Coco called it. Coco also designed the packaging for No. 5: and here again her genius shines through – pure, austere, minimalist, the bottle is hailed as a 20th century design icon.

Karl Lagerfeld took over as artistic director for Chanel in 1983. A worthy successor to Coco, he respects her original rebellious philosophy so much that he is never afraid to reinvent her designs, borrowing from her combination of boldness and subtlety but always adding a pinch of his own wit. Lagerfeld believes "not too much respect and a little bit of humour are indispensable for the survival of a legend." He gives familiar Chanel staples such as the tweed suit, the jersey dress, the chain belt, the camellia and the two-tone shoes a slick update with every collection, reacting intuitively to the speed of the changing times.

Quality is foremost, whether it is the materials used in Chanel's couture collections, or of the craftsmanship and detail behind Chanel watches, bags, make-up products and perfumes.

Chanel's more than 100 boutiques, recently redesigned by American architect Peter Marino, follow the same rules: faithfulness to the Chanel spirit without being constrained by it, continuing Coco's tradition of harmony and minimalism, allowing breathing space for products – and customers.

Coco Chanel would have been delighted to see her successors take her designs and redefine them for the 21st century, while always remaining true to her philosophy of revolution in pursuit of understated elegance.

chanel.co.uk

Registered Trade Mark

A true modern day icon

Coca-Cola continues to be as relevant today as when it was first launched in 1886. Coca-Cola has become one of the world's most recognised and trusted brands through its ability to connect with consumers emotionally and physically.

The enduring brand values of Coca-Cola (authenticity, optimism and bringing people together) come from values people aspire to in their own lives. This is what continues to make Coca-Cola such an icon brand.

Coca-Cola is available in more than 200 countries and is committed to ensuring that the brand should always be 'within arm's reach of desire' providing people with its unique refreshment. As the second most widely understood word in the world, after 'OK', it is easily the most famous and the world's favourite soft drink.

The brand's history of marketing has been legendary; for instance in 1915 the creation of the iconic 'Contour' bottle which was designed so that consumers would recognise it as a Coca-Cola bottle, even if they felt it in the dark. The brand has also been famous for some iconic advertising from the Company's first ever global ad 'Hilltop' to the support of major international sponsorships such as The FIFA World Cup.

Local advertising has continued to keep the brand relevant to consumers worldwide. In March 2004, the first ad in the 'Real World of Coca-Cola' campaign, 'I Wish', was aired in Great Britain and subsequently in the US. Sharlene Hector, a young, up-and-coming British singer, who released her first single in March 2004, delivers the simple but inspirational message that one person can inspire others and bring people together by sharing bottles of Coca-Cola. She sings the classic track, 'I Wish', originally recorded by iconic singer Nina Simone.

So how does the world's most famous brand continue to innovate and surprise consumers in the 21st century? What continues to make the brand so relevant is its ability to tap into consumers' passions and lifestyles in a way that no other brand can.

Music and football are two platforms which Coca-Cola uses to touch people. In 2004 the brand launched the UK's first consumer-branded, legitimate downloadable music site – www.mycokemusic.com. This was a result of research by Coca-Cola that identified that not only was this the future of how consumers will access music, but that they also want to do this from a brand they trust.

The innovative site went live in 2004 and features more than 250,000 new and old tracks. Seven weeks after its launch the site became the biggest retailer of downloadable music in Europe, receiving more hits than any other legal download site.

To support www.mycokemusic.com, Coca-Cola gave consumers the chance to win one of 20 million downloads from the site featured on 200 million packs of Coca-Cola. In the first week, the site received 1,100 hits per hour.

For more than 30 years Coca-Cola has been a committed supporter of football at all levels in Great Britain – from grassroots and sponsorship of ITV's 'The Premiership' to the UEFA European Championships™ and FIFA World Cup™.

In February 2004, The Football League agreed the largest title sponsorship in its history with Coca-Cola Great Britain. As the oldest League in world football, formed in 1888, it's the original that all other football leagues are modelled on, giving Coca-Cola the opportunity to connect with real fans of real football. In addition, as Official Euro 2004 partner, Coca-Cola has teamed up with a number of world class strikers including England's Wayne Rooney, who will also be actively involved in supporting the brand's grassroots schools programme – the 'Coca-Cola' U13s National Schools Cup.

Coca-Cola continues to drive innovative interpretations of its brand and has established strong links within the world of fashion and design. In 2002, Coca-Cola Great Britain challenged five contemporary designers to produce limited edition designs which drew inspiration from the iconic glass bottle. In 2003, the designer Matthew Williamson gave his interpretation of how the iconic bottle would look in one of his trademark summer prints.

In 2004, Matthew Williamson created limited edition Coca-Cola bottles – 'The Summer Icon Collection'. These were based on his own Spring/Summer Couture 2004 designs.

Coca-Cola is a timeless icon – the bottle, the name, the branding – all are firmly embedded in modern culture locally and globally while remaining true to its heritage and promise to offer a simple moment of refreshment.

coca-cola.co.uk

Coutts

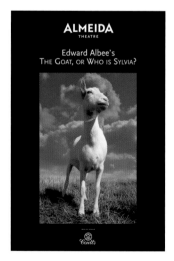

Combining innovative financial solutions with outstanding service for its diverse and fascinating client base has been at the heart of Coutts, the UK's leading private bank, since 1692.

In a business where discretion is paramount, Coutts has always been happy to be less famous than its clients – Charles Dickens and Chopin to name just two. The client base today is just as enviable – industry captains, the up-and-coming professionals of tomorrow and the sports and entertainment personalities of today.

Coutts founder, John Campbell, opened for business on London's Strand under the 'sign of the Three Crowns', an enduring part of Coutts brand mark. The Strand remains its headquarters' home, and the current site's interior was London's first atrium-style building.

It was Thomas Coutts who is credited with having established the values that still drive Coutts today. He also nurtured relationships with the rich and powerful, including William Pitt, Sir Joshua Reynolds and King George III.

In 2000, Coutts became part of The Royal Bank of Scotland Group and consequently has the strength of one of the world's largest banks backing it.

The Coutts Group looks after £65 billion of assets for 90,000 clients. Services span banking, investment, trust, tax and estate planning solutions. The universal belief is that products and their delivery must be 'in their clients' worlds'. In the UK, private bankers are dedicated to looking after clients in similar walks of life, giving them the insight to provide solutions tailored for each client.

Expert Wealth Management for Private Clients

Whilst Coutts roots may be British, the Bank has an international outlook too, with offices in Asia, Europe, the Middle East and offshore jurisdictions.

Coutts has always offered innovation; from bespoke financial solutions for a single client to being the first British private bank with a fully computerised accounting system. The approach to products is no less groundbreaking. Since 1999, its investment programmes have given investors access to a blend of world-leading investment managers – an option usually reserved for institutional investors.

Coutts sponsorship programme includes the Welsh National Opera and the Royal Opera House, but since 2003 it has also been principal sponsor of the Almeida Theatre.

It is this combination of the expected and the unexpected that affords Coutts its cool status. It provides intrigue, without losing sight of its centre of gravity. It allows Coutts to evolve without damaging the heart of a very special brand, which has emotional as well as functional appeal. Providing clients with something that money can't buy is a theme that Coutts is determined to deliver, whether it's going an extra mile in terms of service, hosting Forum 440, a successful entrepreneurs' networking forum established by Coutts, or arranging a client supper with the Royal Opera House's brightest stars.

Coutts promotional strategy is therefore probably most noticeable for its quietness. In a business that's all about relationships, there are no better ambassadors of a brand than satisfied clients. Despite this quiet approach, Coutts enjoys prestigious accolades, such as awards from the international directory, Private Asset Managers, for 'Best Use of Long Only Multi Manager Structures, High Net Worth Class' in 2003 and 2004, and 'Image and reputation' in 2003. In 2004 Coutts was also awarded top place in seven categories of the Euromoney awards, as well as the overall award of the UK's best private bank.

Coutts is as proud of its heritage as it is passionate about its future. Its chequebook is as much an icon of the brand as many other luxury brands' signature products. Its personality is timeless and enduring, whilst being relevant and evolving in a fast changing financial world and, more importantly, in tandem with its clients' worlds.

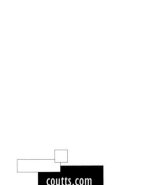
coutts.com

DAZED
& CONFUSED

Defining the cutting edge of culture

Dazed & Confused magazine is the leading independent voice for contemporary creative culture, tapping into new talent to combine original ideas, incisive writing and stunning photography and design. Over the last ten years Dazed has grown from irregularly produced London street zine to internationally revered monthly and respected brand. All the while staying true to the original philosophy – developed by co-founders Jefferson Hack and Rankin – of balancing the aspirational with the inspirational.

As well as offering the most reliable barometer for the shape of things to come in music, film, fashion, art and design, Dazed is not afraid to go in-depth and tackle the social and political issues relevant to young people the world over. In refusing to conform to the product and celebrity-led editorial cycles most magazines adhere to, Dazed has earned the trust of some of the most discerning and savvy consumers of contemporary culture on the planet. In short, Dazed is progressive, influential, optimistic, radical and irreverent. Dazed sets trends, creates stars, provokes controversy and has inspired many pale imitations – but all of that is just a side-effect of the business in hand, which is keeping its readers – and its own staff – entertained, informed, challenged and one step ahead of the game.

At Dazed's core is a team of individually respected editors, writers, stylists, designers and photographers with expert specialist knowledge and an extended family of world class contributors to call upon.

As it has grown in stature and reach, Dazed has begun reinforcing its aims through a series of carefully considered and highly successful brand extensions. Furthering the magazine's longstanding tradition of spring-boarding new talent, four years ago Dazed launched The Re:Creation Awards, in association with Topshop. With categories for Music, Writing, Photography, Film, Fashion Design, Graphics and Illustration, the awards have already helped launch the careers of many exciting new talents and the associated promotional tour has seen

seminar speakers including Zandra Rhodes, Katherine Hamnett, Sir Peter Blake and Anthony H Wilson visit eight different UK cities to offer guidance and inspiration.

The Dazed & Confused aesthetic and ethos has also been successfully exported into the moving image, with the launch in 1998 of Dazed Film & TV. The division has since created award winning programming for Channel 4, FilmFour, BBC TV, five, and is currently in pre-production on Rankin's first feature film.

With the continued success of luxury fashion title, Another Magazine, the Dazed Group has become the first publishing company in the world to successfully balance the innovation of the style magazine with the sophistication of an up-market bi-annual title. Edited in London, art directed from New York, no other magazine allows the reader to get so intimate with the otherwise unapproachable, or lavishes such outstanding, influential image making on such a diverse range of subject matter.

Dazed & Confused has never shied away from challenging conventions and has made a habit of covering topics otherwise considered beyond the scope of the 'style press'. Dazed has been pivotal in supporting initiatives such as Jubilee 2000's Drop The Debt Campaign, the Red Cross' European Youth Projects, the National Blood Association's Give Blood appeal and, most recently with its South Africa issue, the International Aids Vaccine Initiative and African Solutions for African Problems (ASAP) project.

Dazed entered the 21st century having remained in touch with its original risk-taking independent ideals. The magazine is now sold in more than 40 markets worldwide, has a Japanese language co-edition, a book division and continues to further establish itself as the global voice for cutting-edge creative talent.

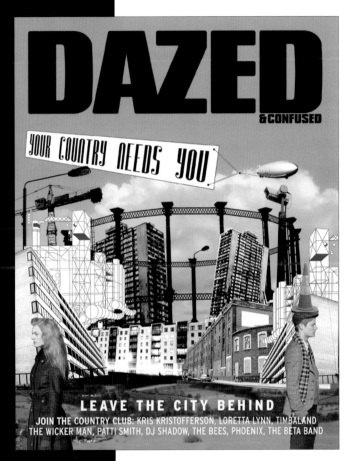

confused.co.uk

DENON

Stylish technology delivering the highest
quality sound and vision.

Denon is a brand built on original ideas and respected for its superb quality hi-fi, Home Cinema, DJ and Pro-Audio equipment, products that bring precision, clarity and high-definition to music and movies, studios, clubs and homes.

Denon customers are rewarded with the pride of ownership that comes from over 75 years of the highest quality engineering and outstanding technical innovation. Today, the brand is recognised internationally as a leading manufacturer for the professional entertainment industries and for discerning individuals.

The Denon brand was established in the 1930s and initially developed turntables and disc recorders for radio stations. In this role, Denon introduced the world's first direct-drive studio turntable in 1939.

Through the 1950s and 1960s, Denon became synonymous with top sound quality among audiophiles and professionals. In 1951 came the launch of the world's first stereo moving coil phono cartridge, marking Denon as the pioneer in high-fidelity (hi-fi) manufacturing. Denon's technological edge was further sharpened in the 1970s when its engineers developed the first practical eight-channel digital recorder and pioneered PCM Digital Recording. As a natural follow-on, in the 1980s the brand was among the very first to introduce CD players and the world's first commercially available CDs to an excited international market. In 1991 Denon created the market, which it still dominates, for delivering superb high-quality miniature hi-fi systems, now followed by stylish home cinema variants.

With the digital entertainment revolution, Denon earned further international acclaim and recognition by applying its high-grade audio technology to the new area of home cinema. Its latest products bring new levels of video quality to DVDs and a sonic realism which literally envelops the listener. In fact, Denon has been the first to bring almost every new leading-edge home cinema technology to market.

In the UK, Denon has grown from zero in 1983 to a position as one of the strongest and most respected brands in the quality market, garnering a string of industry and consumer awards along the way. Denon DJ CD players have become the industry standard for clubs, while its professional products are used in radio stations and studios the world over. During 2003 and 2004, Denon's consumer range received an unprecedented stream of 5* reviews, Best Buys and Best of the Best Awards.

This year, the iconic D-M31 micro hi-fi won the What Hi-fi 'Best Hi-fi' Award for the third year running. And, even as Cool BrandLeaders goes to press, magazines are carrying rave reviews of Denon's hottest new product, the 3805 Advanced Home Cinema Receiver.

As well as producing the best and some of the most expensive home cinema components, Denon also sells huge quantities of the highest quality micro and mini hi-fi and AV systems. The brand, therefore, is built on the quality of its products, which are universally recognised and highly rated around the world by knowledgeable opinion formers, professional users and enthusiasts alike.

Word of mouth is more important than mega marketing campaigns, and Denon consistently dazzles with the excellence of its product, not the size of its advertising spend. And, in an increasingly downmarket world, Denon's success proves that quality still counts.

denon.co.uk

dermalogica®

Innovative formulations and
treatments that work

It's been said that there is nothing as powerful as an idea
whose time has come. This is proven daily by Dermalogica,
the 'quiet revolution' in skincare, with a cult following
ranging from professional skin therapists to Hollywood
makeup artists.

The company was founded in Los Angeles in 1986 by
Jane and Raymond Wurwand, who in 1983 had founded
The International Dermal Institute, the post-graduate
training facility for professional skin therapists which sets
the industry standard for education. Today, all Dermalogica
products are researched and developed by The
International Dermal Institute.

After establishing The International Dermal Institute,
Jane concluded that no available skincare line was suitable
for use in her classrooms; developing her own product
was clearly the next step. It had to be compatible with
her exacting educational standards, and had to meet the
needs of the skincare professionals who would be its sole
means of distribution.

Jane's vision was clear: a product line which was free of
the common irritants which ultimately led to skin
sensitisation, and which was selected and recommended by
a professional skin therapist with the same care that a
physician would prescribe medication. This meant eliminating
mineral oil, S.D. alcohol, artificial colours, artificial fragrances,
lanolin, and formaldehyde – all accepted staple ingredients in
many leading brands at the time.

When Jane first presented her proposals to industrial
chemists, they told her it couldn't be done. Ultimately, one
chemist was able to produce the formulations to Jane's
exacting standards. A few products were developed initially
– Dermal Clay Cleanser, Active Moist, Skin Smoothing
Cream, Special Cleansing Gel, Multi Active Toner – and
the Dermalogica brand was born. The brand's best-sellers
are among this now-classic group of cleansers,
conditioners and moisturisers.

Today, Dermalogica leads the industry by creating
innovative products which conventional manufacturers
would never attempt to formulate. Because the company
is driven by research and education, Dermalogica often
anticipates industry or consumer trends. Advanced
research into new ingredient and product formulation

technologies and an intimate knowledge of the needs of skincare professionals allows the company to develop definitive products well ahead of the consumer 'curve'. As a result, Dermalogica's products addressing acneic, environmentally sensitised, mature and sun-damaged skin, as well as other conditions requiring professional treatment, have consistently been major innovators in these categories.

From the beginning, Dermalogica and its users have consciously held themselves apart from the beauty industry. The company believes in the health and well-being of body, mind and spirit; looking good is a pleasant effect of improved wellness. With this mindset, the brand has never been packaged or marketed with luxury or glamour in mind.

Today, as in the early 1980s, Dermalogica emphasises innovation, information, and education. Products have functional, informative names, not whimsical marketing-driven ones. Packaging is sleek, spare, and designed to reduce contamination and control product application. Dermalogica is the most selected brand among professional skincare therapists in the UK. More than 3,000 skincare centres in the UK alone carry the line, with thousands more in the US, Asia and Australia. Dermalogica does not buy advertising, preferring to gain awareness through word-of-mouth. Likewise, the brand is deliberately not sold in any of the usual retail venues: instead, it is available exclusively through professional skin centres.

In an industry of 'me too' brands, Dermalogica remains unmistakably distinct, interested in real innovation for real results. Rather than launch a dozen new products each year, Dermalogica may launch only one or two, and only when absolutely confident that they will be the best, most effective in their category.

dermalogica.com

DESIGN MUSEUM

Nurturing and showcasing
excellence in design

Design has never been more exciting. At a time when the way we lead our lives is changing dramatically, thanks to advances in technology, everyone wants – and needs – to know how innovative designers are creating the new objects, networks and spaces we will need to live more enjoyably and efficiently in the future. The best place to find out is the Design Museum.

By combining the most ingenious – and seductive – innovations in contemporary design with intriguing insights into design history, the Design Museum has emerged as one of London's most dynamic museums, described by the Financial Times as "the premier advocate and judge of good design." By championing excellence in design – from architecture, fashion and furniture, to cars, graphics and multimedia – the Design Museum shows how great design can enhance every area of our lives with its beauty, functionality, environmental sensitivity or by making us laugh.

The Design Museum is the place where you can find out what the most influential designers of our time – such as Jonathan Ive of Apple, creator of the iPod and iMac, and Marc Newson, whose alluringly futuristic style is imitated worldwide – are planning for the future. Meanwhile, the Designer of the Year award has become the UK's leading design prize by celebrating the richness of our design talent.

As well as presenting the first museum exhibitions of superstar designers – from Manolo Blahnik with his irresistibly sexy shoes and Philip Treacy's spectacular hats to Peter Saville's classic album covers – the Design Museum hosts talks by

grandees such as architects Zaha Hadid and Norman Foster and powerful corporate designers like J Mays of Ford and BMW's Chris Bangle.

Equally innovative is the way the Design Museum presents design to the public. Convinced that museums should be as entertaining as they are educative, the Design Museum strives to ensure that all its exhibitions are as interactive as possible, with visitors trying the designs for themselves rather than simply looking at them. Leading designers participate in every area of activity, including children's creativity workshops (described by The Independent as "innovative and sophisticated... a leap forward") where children are shown how to design and make hats by Philip Treacy and leather bags by Bill Amberg.

One of the Design Museum's most important roles is to nurture new design talent. Through exhibitions, new design commissions and the website, the museum showcases the work of talented young designers to industry, the media and the public. 20 talented young British designers are given the chance to show their work at the guerilla exhibition Design Mart, presented during 100% Design in September, when the design world flocks to London. The Great Brits exhibition of future design superstars, presented at Paul Smith's Milan headquarters during the Milan Furniture Fair, is touring around the world.

As a model modern museum, the Design Museum is not confined to its building: spectacular though it is on the riverfront beside Tower Bridge with sensational views of the City and Canary Wharf. The award-winning Design Museum website – at www.designmuseum.org – is the world's most popular design site. Hundreds of thousands of people seek out innovative multimedia design in the Digital Design Museum and learn more about design history in the online research archive.

The Design Museum's future plans are even more exciting. With soaring visitor numbers, critically acclaimed exhibitions touring to other museums worldwide and a dynamic education programme, the Design Museum is poised for expansion – nationally and internationally. Thanks to a recent increase in government funding and the inspired support of its corporate partners, the Design Museum is perfectly positioned to fulfil its mission of "exciting everyone about design".

designmuseum.org

DIESEL®

FOR SUCCESSFUL LIVING

Unpredictable, dynamic vitality and energy guided by imagination and passion

Diesel's design ethic is not to follow established trends and is largely unaffected by fashion fads; innovative and at times a bit radical, it always pays careful attention to detail and focuses on quality materials and production techniques. It is this obsessive behaviour that is helping Diesel to obtain the position of the 'Pret a Porter of casualwear'. The brand is now present in over 80 countries with more than 250 single-brand stores. It has also attracted some very desirable followers – award-winning hip hop producer Pharrell Williams and actresses Scarlett Johansson and Keira Knightley are fans.

The Diesel brand was created by the Italian duo Renzo Rosso and Adriano Goldschmeid in 1978. The name was chosen because the word means exactly the same thing worldwide – an early indication of the company's international aspirations. Diesel launched with a menswear collection in 1979, and by the early 1980s it was already creating a buzz outside its Italian home market. In 1985, Rosso bought out his partners and became the sole force behind the brand. Thereafter, the company began a period of remarkable growth.

A womenswear line was introduced in 1989, and two years later Diesel launched its global marketing strategy, with the slogan 'For Successful Living'. Other brand extensions, such as Diesel Kids, followed. One extension, 55DSL, an urban fashion collection for men and women, was so successful that although still under the Diesel umbrella it is now run as an independent company, with Andrea Rosso, Renzo's son, as creative director.

Renzo also owns a manufacturer, Staff International, which makes the men's and women's catwalk collections, Dsquared2, and he recently acquired a majority stake in Martin Margiela.

Diesel's Denim Gallery, a premium denim line of limited edition designs and washes, launches in the UK this year, exclusively through Selfridges and Harvey Nichols. It was previously only available from special Denim Gallery stores in New York and Tokyo.

Other offshoots include the art deco Pelican Hotel on Miami's renowned South Beach, celebrating its tenth anniversary this year. Rooms have their own distinctive décor reflected by names such as 'Best Little Whorehouse'

and 'Me Tarzan You Vain'. Johnny Depp, Cameron Diaz and Yoko Ono are among the celebrities who have stayed there.

Rosso also created Diesel Farm nearly ten years ago. Situated in Italy's Marostica Hills, it produces Rosso di Rosso and Bianco di Rosso wines and extra virgin oil.

Rosso has raked in a string of awards, and was ranked number five in The Face magazine's 'Top 100 Most Influential People in Fashion'. Italy's most prestigious MBA programme described Diesel as "an entrepreneurial phenomenon".

The brand's truly original advertising campaigns began in 1991 and changed the world of youth communication overnight. Diesel's ironic appropriation of 1950s advertising vocabulary – suggesting that its products make for a better life – was initially dismissed by traditional marketing 'experts', but has proved an enduring and much-emulated theme. The Cannes Lions (the ultimate advertising award), Eurobest, Epica and onedotzero are just some of the advertising and creative festivals that have showered awards on Diesel over the years. The brand's creative approach doesn't stop with advertising – even its clothing catalogues are considered collectors items for their radical look, with products often serving only as incidental content in a highly stylised publication.

Diesel also encourages the creative talents of the future through projects such as: Diesel-u-music, a competition for up and coming musicians; International Talent Support – IT'S# – a fashion competition for students and young designers; the Raindance Film Festival in London; and Art Now – in association with Tate Gallery.

Rosso, who remains the driving force behind Diesel, is still passionate about the brand he has nurtured. He simply says: "Diesel is not my company – it is my life."

Diet Coke has been instrumental in influencing consumer trends and in the growth in the consumption of diet and low calorie drinks by both men and women around the world.

The launch of diet Coke in 1982 marked the first brand extension of the Coca-Cola brand. By 1990 diet Coke had grown to become the second biggest soft drink in Great Britain and is now sold worldwide in 149 countries. In response to evolving consumer trends The Coca-Cola Company launched Caffeine Free diet Coke in 1988 and for the multitude of people who enjoy a slice of lemon in their diet Coke – diet Coke with Lemon in 2002. The most recent innovation came with the launch of diet Coke Vanilla in 2003.

Diet Coke advertising earned its place in history with the now legendary 'diet Coke break' ads which ran in the late 1990s. The ads, considered revolutionary at the time, reversed the traditional male/female roles by employing a scantily clad diet Coke hunk as the lead and casting the female stars in the predatory role. Still fondly remembered today, the ads confirmed diet Coke's positioning as a modern, sexy brand with a wicked sense of humour.

The '11:30 diet Coke break' TV ads launched with 'Builder' in 1996 featuring a well-toned model, as a builder taking his 11:30am 'diet Coke break' outside a busy office of female admirers.

The ad captured the nation's attention and was followed in 1997 with 'Delivery' starring a new diet Coke hunk entering an office via the lift, again at 11:30am, to deliver a case of diet Coke to an office of drooling females. The ad series finale came with 'Appointment', which aired in 1998 and featured a sexy office window cleaner. 'Appointment' became a British viewer's favourite, receiving a National Television Award in 1998 for 'Best Television Commercial'.

The 'Hunk' ads evolved into the 'Matthew & Jennifer' campaign in 2000. The ads looked at the quirky rituals of

Makes your break more like play time

Must be a Diet Coke thing.

'break-time' at work and the indulgence in gossip, love, flirtation and mischief of its five central characters.

Diet Coke's advertising continued to evolve throughout 2002 adding more fun, light-hearted campaigns to its now historical reel. In June 2003 diet Coke launched a major new TV campaign using the strapline 'It must be a diet Coke thing'. The most recent ad 'Mannequin' shows two female window dressers taking a sneaky diet Coke break. One of the girls playfully twangs a male mannequin's pants causing it to lose balance. This leads to a domino-type collapse ending with the mannequins in somewhat compromising positions.

An association with movies in 2003, showed the more glamorous side to diet Coke's personality.

The programme kicked off with The diet Coke Movie Weekend and included sponsorship of West End film premieres and a TV ad starring Hollywood actress Kim Basinger.

The movie programme continued in 2004 with the diet Coke Film Fest – a national promotion to find the nation's favourite films, to be shown back-to-back on the big screen in one weekend.

Through its movies association, diet Coke had raised its glamour quotient, but this wasn't the first time that the brand had forged aspirational partnerships. In September 2003 diet Coke linked up with high end jewellery designer Theo Fennel to produce stunning bottles in sterling silver. The limited edition bottles promoted the 'silver spree' campaign which offered consumers the chance to win high value spending sprees.

Diet Coke's most recent innovation is the launch of the Mini Break can – a 250ml for people who want quick refreshment on the go.

Today, diet Coke retains the spirit of the diet Coke break in everything that it does – a moment to escape the humdrum of everyday life, let go and have some fun.

dietcoke.co.uk

DUST

Inspired by design, music and energy

The Dust name is linked to the passage of time, and was inspired by the bar's location in Clerkenwell, an area long associated with London's watch making industry. One truth in which all can trust is that London will turn to Dust. And so it has – to drink, eat and dance in an atmosphere ruled by design, music and an innate sense of occasion.

The Dust concept dates back to 1995 when the founders, Ray Brown and Mark Thompson, met on a design course at North London University. They were bored of their day jobs and were driven by a passion to create a new style of bar in the evolving East London scene. Upon graduating, they found the ideal space for their concept – a derelict Victorian factory building. They set about converting it into a stylish watering hole where people would want to spend their time. Unusually, the two undertook all the design and most of the construction work themselves. From the shell of the factory, Dust took shape. In 2002, a new management team led by Jon Ross was brought in to inject fresh energy into the brand.

As well as being a watch making centre, Clerkenwell was also a water supply centre for the capital; water and time provided broad design themes for the bar. The original character of the building has been preserved through the restoration of wooden floors, brick walls, tongue-and-groove panelling and cast iron support beams. In the basement is a circular lobby, inspired by a subterranean well.

The front of the bar has an intimate feel, with a low ceiling, comfortable sofas and chunky tables. At the back of the ground floor, the roof consists entirely of a skylight at first floor level, creating a double-height space in which the rear wall is covered in copper leaf. Thoughtful lighting, earthy colours and natural materials complete the look, whilst original artwork is displayed throughout and changes every month. Dust opened in the summer of 1998. Clean and simple lines and careful attention to detail have ensured that, six years on, the design still feels fresh.

Dust has evolved and flourished under the direction of the current management team, Jon Ross, Alistair Priddle and Shane Gavin. They have instinctively streamlined and updated the brand, procuring a late licence to allow devotees to sling back seasonal cocktails until 4am, and developing a fine portfolio of DJs to man the decks. Quality music has been important to the brand from its inception, but now Dust regularly brings breaking talent to the public, with new DJs supporting well-known names. The style of music varies from night to night, but the mantra for the smiling, discerning crowd remains the same: drink in the atmosphere, dance off your worries and trust in Dust.

The brand is expanding. The addition of a first floor bar in the autumn of 2002 gave Dust an extra dimension. Now groups can hire space to savour their own private Dust experience, making for a truly special corporate or personal celebration. 2003 saw Dust visiting Westbourne Grove, with its own venture into the sound system maelstrom that is Notting Hill Carnival. A regular outing at the event is now part of the calendar. Further schemes, both on home turf and abroad, are already crystallising for 2004.

Dust is moving forward with independent, infectious energy. Pure enjoyment.

dustbar.co.uk

GAGGIA®

La crème de la crème of coffee machines

MACCHINA TIPO ESPORTAZIONE "6 GRUPPI"

As any coffee connoisseur will tell you, espresso is all about the 'crema'. This is the delicate, unbroken, golden-brown foam that covers the surface of every perfect espresso, obscuring the powerful black core of the coffee beneath, and we owe the creation of the 'crema' to Gaggia.

Achille Gaggia unveiled his first coffee machine on September 5th 1938. It was his ingenious idea of forcing water under pressure to flow over the coffee grounds – instead of the usual method of blasting them with steam – that produced this 'crema'.

Gaggia went on to officially found his coffee machine company in 1947, and since then the brand has become synonymous throughout the world with authentic Italian coffee. Over the years the machines have evolved from the traditional manually operated devices, with a lever controlling a water-pressurising piston, to fully automated marvels that can grind, measure and deliver a delicious cup of espresso at the flick of a switch.

A crucial chapter in the development of the brand came with the introduction of the Baby Gaggia in 1977. The first domestic coffee machine, its launch capitalised on the rise in popularity of espresso during the 1970s. For the first time, it was possible to create in your own home an espresso to rival those being sipped in cafés. The Baby Gaggia established the brand at the forefront of the domestic machine market, a position it retains to this day. All Gaggia machines are made in the Robecco sul Naviglio factory in Milan, and are designed to combine tradition with technology.

Three of the latest Gaggia machines are The Titanium, The Baby D and Achille Gaggia.

The Titanium is a fully automated coffee machine offering advanced bean to cup technology – with just a press of one button, The Titanium grinds the beans, measures the coffee and brews straight into the cup. Encased in sleek stainless steel and designed with the gourmet gadget lover in mind, this state-of-the-art espresso machine is elegant, robustly-built and essentially created for the home and small offices.

Baby D is a stylish espresso machine equipped with an innovative dosing system that lets you set the amount of coffee that goes into the cup just the way you like it – all you have to do is press the coffee button and your baby will memorise just how to make your favourite cup of coffee.

The founder of Gaggia is honoured by the company he created by having a product named after him: the Achille Gaggia coffee maker unites vintage aesthetics with technology of the future. Exceptional features include a complete stainless steel structure, with a pressure gauge and traditional coffee lever, combined with unparalleled performance.

Proudly displayed in restaurants and bars across the globe, gleaming Gaggia machines prove their worth and act as their own marketing tools. But the brand also has a trade communications programme to raise awareness of new and existing products. As well as issuing press materials and photographs, the company regularly loans out machines to trade shows and magazine reviewers and enjoys media coverage which spans consumer and trade publications, radio and television broadcasts, and online media.

Gaggia's reputation, however, has primarily been built through quality, design – and a passion for making the perfect espresso, every time.

gaggia.uk.com

Goldsmiths
UNIVERSITY
OF LONDON

A hothouse of creative talent

Britain, and particularly London, is central to the international contemporary cultural scene – a breeding ground for creativity and the creative industries – and nowhere more so than Goldsmiths College. Situated in South East London, Goldsmiths is well-known for its high academic standards and for the individuals who have blossomed as a result of the Goldsmiths experience.

Part of the University of London, Goldsmiths has a reputation for nurturing some of the finest creative talents over the years. Think Mary Quant, Bridget Riley, Malcom McLaren, Antony Gormley, John Cale, Blur, Damian Hirst, Sarah Lucas, Julian Opie, Molly Parkin, Gillian Wearing – the list goes on.

Founded in 1891 and part of the University of London since 1904, Goldsmiths' reputation precedes it – particularly in the arts, education, social sciences and humanities. The College offers a broad range of undergraduate, postgraduate, professional and adult education programmes and currently has around 10,000 students from around the world.

Key to its success is the liberal and creative approach taken in the teaching of all subjects, not just the arts, along with the emphasis it places on teaching led by pioneering research across all areas of study and departments. Goldsmiths is part of the prestigious '94 Group' of smaller research-oriented universities, committed to international standards of excellence. The College did extremely well in the most recent quality assessment of its research, with Media and Communications and Sociology receiving the highest possible rating, ranking them amongst the best.

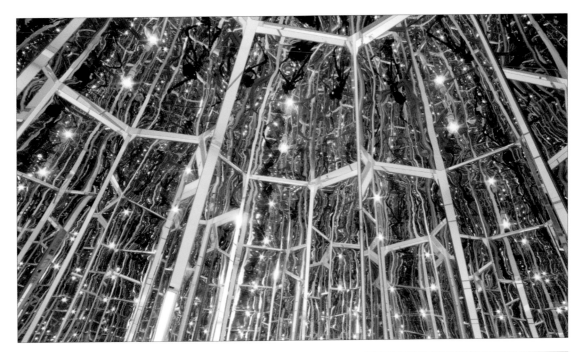

Goldsmiths has defined artistic movements for many generations and is regarded by many as the most innovative university for the creative arts in Europe. Contemporary galleries such as Tate Modern are bursting with the work of Goldsmiths alumni. Since it began over ten years ago, four winners of the Turner Prize – and almost a quarter of those shortlisted for the award – have been Goldsmiths graduates. Past students have also been credited with starting the Young British Artists 'YBA' movement.

But it's not just Visual Arts: Goldsmiths also has excellent Music, Drama and English Departments, covering the whole spectrum of creative arts teaching.

Goldsmiths' creative ethos is also reflected in its promotional materials, which have won over fifteen national and international PR and marketing awards in recent years, making it the most prolific award-winner of any UK university.

In order to continue its high standards, a stunning new building, designed by Alsop Architects, is under way on campus. This will house state-of-the-art teaching space and studios, as well as a new Centre for Cognition, Computation and Culture, which, together with Digital Studios, will bring together science, new technology, digital media, the arts and social sciences in a research facility unique in the UK.

goldsmiths.ac.uk

Arthur Guinness (1725-1803) might have thought that fathering 21 children was more than enough to guarantee the survival of his family name. Who could have foreseen that his buying a disused Dublin brewery in 1759 would also have founded a global brewing empire which, more than 200 years later, ensured that his name was known around the world?

Buoyed by a £100 legacy from his godfather, the 27-year-old left the small brewery where he had been working in County Kildare, and headed for the Irish capital. There he rented the St. James's Gate Brewery, shrewdly paying £45 a year for a 9,000-year lease – and Guinness beer is still brewed there today.

But competition was fierce when Arthur set up. There were 200 breweries in Ireland, ten in St James's Gate alone. Fuelled by self-belief and determination, Arthur began production of Guinness Original beer, a carbonated stout (known then as porter). By 1794, Guinness Irish Porter was being exported to England and, by 1802, it had reached the West Indies. Three of Arthur's sons entered the business and galvanised the export drive, with the result that by the end of the 19th century the Guinness brewery was the largest in the world. The first Guinness brewery outside of the British Isles was in Nigeria in 1961: today, there are 50 Guinness breweries around the world, and a staggering two billion pints are drunk each year in the 150 countries where it is sold.

Guinness is brewed from just four basic ingredients – barley, water, hops and yeast. The characteristic dark colour of the beer (actually a deep, ruby-red) is created through the use of roasted barley in the brew, which also adds to the richness of the flavour. Even after more than 200 years, every pint of Guinness has an authentic link back to Arthur Guinness' original porter – yeast from each brew is transferred on to the next, so the original yeast's descendants are still in Guinness beer today.

The iconic black beer, with a touch of genius

GUINNESS
EXTRA COLD

ILLUSTRATOR FAIYAZ JAFRI

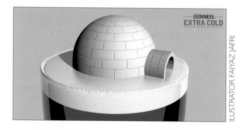

Never compromising on quality or straying from Arthur Guinness' legacy, Guinness has nevertheless been an important innovator in the beer industry. The smooth, creamy pint of Guinness Draught we know today was first launched in 1959. This category-changing innovation continued with the introduction of the widget, transporting the perfect Guinness beer into a can in 1989, and Guinness Draught Extra Cold, a decade later.

Almost as well loved as the drink itself, Guinness has a great heritage in advertising with some of the most memorable campaigns of the last century. With most public houses in Britain in the early half of this century owned or 'tied' to a particular brewery, Guinness relied on maintaining a strong level of customer demand to justify its distribution. It was the role of advertising that ensured this demand. From the famous Gilroy Toucan advertisements, débuted in 1935, and the early 'Guinness is good for you' campaigns, through Pure Genius and 'the man with the Guinness', the brand continually broke new ground in advertising, and still does to this day. The 1999 'Surfer' television ad from the 'Good things come to those who wait' campaign was voted the most popular ad ever by the British public in a Sunday Times and Channel 4 poll. Although strikingly different in style over the years, the ads have always been a confident and witty reflection of the unique qualities of the beer itself. The latest campaign 'Out of darkness comes light' continues this tradition.

An essential part of 'the Craic', Guinness stands proud as the confident choice in an increasingly generic beer market.

Guinness.com

ha✕kasan

Exquisite oriental cuisine with a
backdrop of relaxed decadence

Hakkasan was created by Alan Yau with the intention of being the best restaurant around. Its name amalgamates the owner's ethnicity – 'Hakka' are people from the New Territories of Hong Kong – with 'San' being the respectful Japanese form of address. Firmly rooted in traditional Chinese culture, the ethos of the restaurant, which is reflected in its cuisine, is out-going: unafraid to absorb and adapt influences from wherever they may be found. The Hakkasan logo, by North Design, reinforces this identity by employing a clean, modern font that incorporates a back-to-back double K, which echoes the Chinese symbol for good fortune.

Designed by Christian Liaigre, described by The Financial Times as "possibly the most important – certainly the most copied – designer of our age," the dramatic interior is frequently compared to a film set. Visitors are impressed by the contrast between the restaurant's location in an unprepossessing back alley and the glamorous atmosphere they encounter upon descending into the basement premises. This artfully-illuminated subterranean world exemplifies Liaigre's distinctive sensibility, which he summarises as 'luxe, calme, moderne' and other commentators tend to characterise as 'sexy'.

Liaigre has divided what is actually a huge space into two principle areas: a dining room that seats 130, enclosed by Chinese-style lattice screens; and a separate lounge bar, called Ling Ling which is served by a sixteen metre-long bar and animated by a pulsing, customised soundtrack. The luxurious aspect of Liaigre's aesthetic is evoked by his use of high quality materials, such as

the wall of sawn slate behind the bar and the dark-stained English oak from which the mighty bar, tables, and screens are made. These screens provide oblique and unexpected views into and from the dining area, creating a discreet, almost conspiratorial atmosphere in which to enjoy a meal, while promoting a sense of calm by separating the dining area from the busier, buzzier bar. The lounge area features another of Liaigre's design motifs in the chairs, which are beautifully upholstered in leather and embroidered with dragons. The lighting, by Arnold Chan at Isometrix, adds to the drama.

The style of Hakkasan is exemplified by the waiting staff, who are not necessarily Chinese, but who provide knowledgeable advice to customers who may not have previously encountered such emblematic dishes as Pi Pa duck; sea bass cooked in a clay pot with tofu and aubergine; or fried soft shell crab with garlic chilli and curry leaf.

Although critics have questioned the 'authenticity' of some of the dishes served at Hakkasan, the fact is that the menu is produced and developed by highly-trained Chinese chefs who are eager to extend their repertoire, yet always working within the strict parameters of a cuisine that relies upon the inviolable flavour combinations of sweet and sour, salt and pepper, chilli and garlic. Therefore, the stir-fried ostrich with preserved rice and Shao Hsing wine served at Hakkasan is just as 'Chinese' as Shark's fin soup.

The credit for the culinary invention of Hakkasan must go to Tong Chee Hwee, who arrived as head chef from the renowned Summer Pavilion restaurant at the Ritz Carlton hotel in Singapore. Chef Tong's cooking secured a star in the Michelin Guide for Hakkasan, which remains the only Chinese restaurant in the UK to boast such an accolade. At the Carlton London Restaurant Awards in 2004, Chef Tong was short listed as Chef of the Year and carried off the award for Best Oriental Restaurant of the Year award for the second year running.

Chef Tong's superb dim sum, served at lunchtimes, has proven to be so popular that Alan Yau has now opened a restaurant dedicated to dim sum, Yauatcha.

El Ron de Cuba

The Spirit of Cuba

To enter Cuba is to enter a different way of life. The flavour of rum in your mouth, the aroma of cigars wisping around your nose. The baking sun and the music – music everywhere. On the street corners, in the alleyways, in the bars. Smiling, beautiful people swaying to a rhythm. Life, hardship and dancing. The decaying elegance which is the cradle of the Daiquiri and the home of the Mojito, drunk to a soundtrack of salsa. Another sunset, another night full of spirit, a people full of passion.

Havana Club epitomises Cuba; a country that, as Dave Broom, journalist, author and Rum expert eloquently states, "gets under your skin and into your soul. Walk out of Jose Marti airport at midnight and you are plunged into a steam bath. There are aromas of vegetation, flowers, dust, petrol fumes, sweat and somehow totally bizarrely mint. Maybe it's the mouth twitching in anticipation of the first Mojito." Welcome to El Ron de Cuba – The Rum of Cuba.

Sugar cane, the singular most important raw ingredient for rum, grows better in Cuba's unique climate than anywhere else in the world and, by the 18th century, Cuba was the 'world's sugar reserve'.

Havana Club was born in 1878 with the foundation of the distillery, La Viscaya. By the 1930s, the brand had become a definitive part of Havana's exciting nightlife and drinking repertoire. It is synonymous with legendary bars such as El Floridita and La Bodeguita del Medio in Havana as well as some of their most famous patrons such as Ernest Hemingway, Marilyn Monroe and Humphrey Bogart. Today, Havana Club embodies the spirit of Cuba and is the only truly international Cuban rum brand.

The recipe for Havana Club is a closely guarded secret, so closely protected that only five people in Cuba know the formula. El Maestro Ronero, the rum master, has the key role of ensuring that every bottle delivers consistent quality with a little bit of Havana thrown in for good measure.

The ultimate spirit to mix, Havana Club is an ideal cocktail base and is the only authentic base for the Cuban classics such as the Mojito, the Daiquiri and the Cuba Libre. Its provenance is inherent in its appeal.

The key element of the logo and one of the key brand assets is The Giraldilla. Based on an actual statue cast in 1634, it represents Isabel de Bobadilla of Seville. She sits atop the Castillo de la Real Fueza, constantly awaiting the return of her husband who is yet to come back from his search for eternal youth. This symbol of fidelity and hope has been nicknamed 'Bella Havana' – or beautiful Havana – by the inhabitants of the city, and is a fitting symbol for the rum that epitomises Cuba's capital.

Havana Club has steadily built a loyal following due to its authenticity, quality and of course its inherent representation of Cuban culture. Every bartender who uses any of the rums in the range seems to become an ambassador, extolling the virtues. It is the rum of choice in many of the leading bars in the UK and, arguably, the world.

The brand stands for self discovery, which means that advertising and promotions are low key and based around clever, synergistic associations, in environments that are relevant to all that is passionate, original and representative of quality and authenticity.

Havana Club is currently the number three premium rum brand in the world and ranks 50th in the top 100 premium sprits brands. It was the fastest growing spirit brand in the world between 1997 and 2001 (Source: IWSR).

havana-club.com

innocent
little tasty drinks

Nature's finest stuff, in a bottle

Everything innocent does is made by nature. And that means only using nature's finest ingredients in its drinks, with nothing added whatsoever.

This principal applies to more than just the drinks. Being natural informs every aspect of the company and brand – from the choice of stationery to the fact that whenever you call the banana phone, you'll always speak to a real person. All of innocent's communication is simple and honest and every single person at innocent does their daily business in a way they can feel proud of. The innocent brand is an extension of the love and nature that goes into each drink.

innocent has been making little tasty drinks since 1999. Founders Rich, Jon and Adam had talked about starting a company ever since they met at university. After a couple of false starts, they struck upon the idea of crushing up lots of healthy fruit and sticking it into bottles. They surmised that there were people out there just like them, looking for an instant, natural shot of good health. And, most importantly, one that actually tasted nice, too.

To test out this idea, they bought £500 worth of fruit, turned it into smoothies and sold them from a stall at a little music festival in London in summer 1998. Above their stall was a sign that read 'Do you think we should give up our day jobs?', beneath which was a bin saying 'YES' and a bin saying 'NO'. At the end of the weekend the 'YES' bin was full, so they went to work the next day and resigned.

After selling the first ever 'proper' innocent smoothies in April 1999, the company has grown steadily. And nothing much has really changed. Each innocent smoothie still contains your recommended daily intake of fruit. Fruit Towers has grown to accommodate 50 people who are passionate about what they do, whilst having a bit of fun along the way. And Rich, Jon and Adam are still friends, which is nice.

There are now six smoothie recipes, including an ever-changing seasonal recipe. And innocent has started to make other drinks, such as thickies (bio yoghurt and fruit blends), super smoothies (smoothies designed with a

specific healthy purpose) and juicy water (spring water and fresh juice, surprisingly enough).

The details are very important to innocent. The copy on their labels changes constantly, which enables them to have an ongoing conversation with their drinkers. The bottle caps say 'enjoy by' instead of the standard 'best before'. And they've also done some questionable things to their vehicle fleet, covering ice-cream vans in turf and sticking horns and udders onto their cow vans.

In 2003, innocent decided that it would be a nice idea to say thanks to everyone who'd bought their drinks and helped them since the company began. So they organised Fruitstock, the first ever free music festival to be held in London's Regent's Park. The success of the weekend outstripped all expectation, and 40,000 people went home with sunburnt noses and smiles on their faces. Plans for a bigger, better Fruitstock in 2004 are well underway.

2004 also sees the birth of the innocent foundation, a separate registered charity devoted to finding good things to do with innocent's money, both in the countries where it sells its drinks and in those where it sources its ingredients.

It's been a busy five years, and European expansion beckons. By sticking to one central idea – that of being natural – innocent has achieved great things for a small company and developed a brand that truly seems to strike a chord.

innocentdrinks.co.uk

Land Rover is one of the few brands that can boast a range of iconic products, recognised the world over by their silhouette alone. Launched in 1947 as a stopgap product by the Rover Car Company, the original Land Rover quickly established a ready market for its 'go anywhere' capabilities. Used by farmers and construction companies, armies and explorers, Land Rovers helped open up and develop vast areas of the third world in the 1950s and 1960s.

Defender's iconic shape is now being embraced by a whole new generation of users – the streetwise urban traveller. Dressed with alloy wheels, chequer plate trim and colours never seen before on this erstwhile utility vehicle, editions such as the Defender Black are appealing more than ever to buyers who are design and fashion conscious.

Launched in 1970, Range Rover broke new ground and became the definitive Leisure SUV. Rapturously received for its style and look, Range Rover was quickly adopted by the rural set and country gentry as the must-have vehicle for all occasions. And the design was so admired that a Range Rover body shell was exhibited in the Louvre museum in Paris as a work of art.

Aided by a limited edition in association with Vogue magazine, the Range Rover was progressively pushed further and further upmarket, gaining new devotees in the urban, business and design sectors. 32 years on, the fourth generation Range Rover was launched to international acclaim in 2002. Jeremy Clarkson even claimed the new Range Rover had "the power of a volcano, the presence of God, and is probably the best car in the world."

With the launch of the All New Discovery in 2004, the iconic styling cues which have made Discovery such a success over the last fifteen years are encapsulated in an extremely modern design. With an entirely new Integrated Bodyframe™, a whole host of exciting new technological features and two new engines, All New Discovery is set to redefine the benchmark for Leisure SUV's yet again.

Late 2003 saw a comprehensive update to the Freelander model which re-established it as a front runner in the Compact SUV market. The substantial interior changes and the addition of the Sport model, as well as style orientated special editions such as XEi, have rejuvenated the nameplate and offer a very desirable, accessible entry into the Land Rover brand.

Unlike many brands, Land Rover is a cluster brand, non linear in nature, offering product designs and experiences to discreet areas in the 4x4 marketplace – utility, luxury, urban and leisure. This cluster nature allows each model to appeal to a specific group of customers and facilitates the introduction of additional new product.

Over the years Land Rover's communications have garnered many awards and memorable television advertising campaigns which still have huge recall even today.

Following the success of the inaugural Land Rover G4 Challenge in 2003, this spectacular global adventure competition is set to return in 2005. Working in bi-national teams, men and women representing eighteen nations will pit stamina and skill in an arena stretching across four countries on two continents, over a four-week period in October 2005. Land Rover vehicles form the base of operations for the competitors as they bike, climb, kayak and 4x4 drive their way towards victory and a New Range Rover as their trophy.

landrover.co.uk

L'Artisan Parfumeur

PARIS

Luxurious fragrances inspired by familiar scents from memory's sweetest corners

Founded in 1976, L'Artisan Parfumeur offers a range of delightfully individualistic perfumes, many based on spices, fruits and plants which other perfume houses have yet to explore – so musk is married to blackberries, figs, hazelnuts, even crushed black pepper in a range of fragrances which are inspired by nature and by familiar scents drawn from intensely personal experiences.

Of all the five senses, scent is the one which most immediately triggers memory and emotional response. No surprise, then, that L'Artisan Parfumeur deliberately sets out to create fragrances which evoke some of the most powerful memories a person can have. Childhood, first love, a walk in the woods, a pie baking in the oven, a night at the circus – the inspirations for the company's perfumes over the years have been eclectic, marvelous, idiosyncratic, challenging, audacious, poetic, humorous…

Its latest perfume, launched in summer 2004, is a case in point. Ananas Fizz takes its inspiration from the Victorian's obsession with and love for the pineapple, which they called 'the cactus fruit' and which for them symbolised the promise of a passionate love affair. Produced as a limited edition and presented in a stylish bottle with a charming pineapple neck, Ananas Fizz not only smells sublime, it is also bound to be one of summer 2004's most covetable accessories.

Despite the unusual ingredients found in many of the company's products, the way they are blended together is very traditional. The result is timeless compositions which carry with them an enormous weight of memory, nostalgia, romance, and yet are very much of this moment.

The company is even recognised by its rivals within the perfume industry as a genuine laboratory of ideas, where customers return again and again to experience the latest in fragrance trends. As is only to be expected from a perfume house which leads where others eventually follow, L'Artisan Parfumeur has built up a dedicated following amongst those who know and understand fine perfumes, and famous fans include the likes of Madonna, Catherine Deneuve, Sarah Jessica Parker, Claudia Schiffer, Elle Macpherson and Michelle Pfeiffer.

Many clients are won over by the brand's unprecedented level of service, which includes perfumes tailor-made for them, as well as olfactory workshops and personalised products.

L'Artisan Parfumeur offers a complete range of perfumes for clients to use on themselves or around their homes. Quality is an over-riding concern, and all of the ingredients used are first-class, while the products are displayed to their best advantage in exclusively designed facetted bottles, packaged in black boxes with labels colour coded according to the fragrance.

There are 30 fragrances in the eau de toilette and eau de parfum portfolio, many with associated bath and beauty products including soaps, shower gels and body lotions. For the home, there is a complete range of scented products – room sprays, burning oils and scented candles. Then there are the curiosities range of original scented objects and perfumed-based seasonal collections. All of the product ranges are reinvented and enriched every year.

L'Artisan Parfumeur has two stores in London – one in Beauchamp Place and the other on Cale Street. The company's flagship store in the heart of Paris, La Grande Boutique de L'Artisan Parfumeur, was opened in 2003: it is perfectly situated, adjacent to the Louvre Museum and overlooking the Seine. It encapsulates the brand's attitude to distribution: alternative and exclusive, there are more than 700 worldwide outlets stocking the company's products, ranging from those that bear the L'Artisan name, through counters in the most prestigious specialty stores in the world to corners in the most trendy fashion or gift boutiques.

L'Artisan Parfumeur – world-class expertise in the age-old craft of perfume making, married with the most modern and evocative scents.

artisanparfumeur.com

LAVAZZA
ITALY'S FAVOURITE COFFEE

'Espress Yourself' with Italian sophistication and spirit

As hip and quintessentially Italian as a Rome coffee bar in a Fellini movie, Lavazza has been the driving force behind the growth of the world's love affair with real Italian espresso coffee for more than 100 years. And now, at the dawn of the 21st century, the aroma and quality of Lavazza, Italy's favourite coffee, continue to satisfy existing espresso lovers and make new conquests for the brand.

Lavazza dates back to 1895, when Luigi Lavazza founded The Lavazza Company, an all-purpose grocery store in Turin. Luigi soon realised that the Italian public was crying out for one special product – coffee. He started sourcing the finest raw materials and roasting and selling his own blend, and quickly enjoyed an enviable reputation as a provider of first-class coffees, with customers flocking from miles around to his store.

From the start, Luigi was open to new ideas, whether in terms of technology or business. The company expanded and modernised distribution and was the first Italian firm to deliver fresh coffee on trucks. Later, it introduced the first vacuum packed tins.

Lavazza was a pioneer in marketing, too. In the 1950s, it launched its first image-based advertising campaign using the slogan 'Lavazza: Paradiso in tazza' – paradise in a cup. Soon after, Luigi's marketing-savvy grandson Emilio joined the company, and began the long-running association with leading Italian advertising agency Armando Testa, which still exists today.

Lavazza was an early user of famous personalities in its advertising, including film star Monica Vitti and opera singer Luciano Pavarotti. It was, however, the introduction of the Lavazza calendars in the 1990s that strengthened the brand's cool credentials and the bond between its marketing communications and the world of the arts.

Helmut Newton shot the first in 1993, infusing it with a style, sensuality and vigour that set the template for subsequent shoots. The likes of Ellen Von Unwerth, Elliott Erwitt, Martine Franck, and no less than twelve different photographers from Magnum, the legendary picture

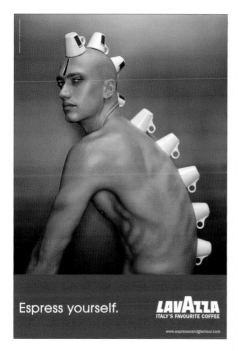

Espress yourself.

LAVAZZA
ITALY'S FAVOURITE COFFEE

www.espressoendglamour.com

Espress yourself.

LAVAZZA
ITALY'S FAVOURITE COFFEE

www.missiontoespresso.com

agency founded by Robert Capa and Henri Cartier-Bresson, have worked with Lavazza.

Since 2002 the calendar shoot has also formed the basis for Lavazza's press and poster advertising. Using the line 'Espress Yourself', reflecting both Lavazza's positioning as the world's leading espresso brand and its commitment to free artistic expression, the 2002 images were conjured up by the controversial David LaChapelle, while the 2003 campaign was shot by Jean-Baptiste Mondino and featured on billboards across Europe.

The 2004 calendar, created by the French fashion photographer Thierry Le Goués, is set on Planet Espresso, where cups are formed out of rock, 'lunar' craters are brimming full of silky espresso and a beautiful, blonde, Barbarella-style astronaut is on a mission to explore.

Powerful and elegant, with an international appeal, the ads reflect the evolution of Lavazza, Italy's favourite coffee, into a global brand.

In the UK, Lavazza continues to display its Italian love of beauty and creativity through its association with the world of art and fashion, which began in 1997 when Lavazza partnered with designer Vivienne Westwood. The brand

is proud to be the Official Coffee to London Fashion Week, serving up little black espresso and cappuccino classics to the cream of the fashion world.

Lavazza also patronises the culinary arts, through its 20-year-old 'laboratory of coffee', the Lavazza Training Centre. In 2003 it teamed up with top International chef Ferran Adrià, famous for the creativity and originality of his ideas, to create 'Espesso' – the world's first solid espresso, which is not drunk, but eaten.

It is through such exciting partnerships that Lavazza is able to continually refresh both itself and coffee lovers around the globe.

lavazza.com

LINN

> The benchmark for performance sound and vision

It surprises many people to learn that the world's finest sound and vision systems are designed and manufactured in Scotland by an independent company called Linn. Founded in 1972 by Ivor Tiefenbrun, Linn did not set out to be the biggest, or the cheapest, or even the most profitable consumer electronics producer – just the best. Ivor dreamt of making a music system that communicated the thrill and emotion of a live performance, and today Linn designs and manufactures an extensive range of award winning music, home theatre and multi-room systems.

All Linn systems, regardless of price, are designed to get as close to the original performance as possible. Precision engineered to ensure the most accurate sound reproduction, Linn systems can be found in the world's finest homes, superyachts, royal palaces and, most recently, Aston Martin cars. Linn's first product, the SONDEK LP12 turntable, was designed and built by Ivor using his experience in precision engineering. It is difficult to appreciate today the profound effect this product had on the hi-fi industry; suffice it to say the SONDEK LP12 re-wrote the rule book.

The LP12 had no flashing lights or controls, just a simple on-off switch; when doubtful shop owners asked Ivor how they could sell it, he replied "Just let your customers hear it". Its performance transformed the sound of any system and from that point on Linn's products have been sold by comparison with competitive products so that customers can judge the sound quality for themselves. The fact the SONDEK LP12 remains in production to this day, and is still referred to

as the most significant hi-fi product ever, is a testimony to the spirit of innovation and free-thinking which remains at Linn. Since that first turntable, Linn has never made a product unless it can make it better than anyone else.

The commitment to producing the world's best quality products is reflected within Linn's purpose-built HQ in the Southside of Glasgow where, instead of a production line, highly skilled individuals build, test and pack complete products by hand before signing their name as a guarantee of quality.

Linn has never courted 'mass market' appeal; instead it has become a brand discovered by people who care enough about quality to actively seek out the best. Linn's status as the performance leader within the industry has largely been achieved through a single-minded determination to do things its own way, a principle demonstrated by its commitment to use only its own original designs. As testament to the success of this commitment, in 2000 the British Design Council selected three of Linn's products as exemplars of British product design for the new Millennium.

Linn's signature promotional style was established throughout the 1980s and 1990s with several high profile advertising campaigns. With some adverts banned immediately upon release, Linn campaigns became renowned for their provocative, tongue-in-cheek headlines which reflected the company's non-conformist and convention-challenging culture. Today, Linn's advertising may be less shocking, but it is no less inventive and it retains Linn's unique sense of humour.

Above all else, through the years Linn has remained a 'hype free' brand which believes that good hi-fi or home theatre has nothing to do with complex specifications or long feature lists. Linn's advice to customers has always been simple: all you have to do is listen – if it sounds better, it is better.

linn.co.uk

Malmaison

The world of Malmaison is a world of contemporary elegance, of style and individuality, of proportion, taste and, yes, drama and theatre. Partly, this is because of the company's attitude to its properties: all of the hotels in the group are sensitively converted from existing buildings – for example, the new Oxford hotel is being carved out of the Victorian prison. Rather than cover over structures' previous 'lives', their history and that of the areas they are in is celebrated in architectural features and original artwork.

And when it comes to the individual rooms, no two rooms across the group look the same, which helps guests forget that they are in a hotel – too often, hotel 'chains' opt for a mass-produced high-style look which is identical, whatever city you are in. Not at a Malmaison: you can expect big beds, power showers, CD players, CD libraries, satellite TV, and funky bars with high quality drinks and interesting snacks.

This is a very deliberate policy: people who travel on business, who make up Malmaison's core market, would always rather be at home than in a hotel, and if the room they are staying in looks like every other hotel room they have been in, there's no chance of truly relaxing.

A hotel has to be a place that people can enjoy being in, rather than endure being in. So the archetypal Malmaison is a small, contemporary hotel close to all the attractions of a busy city centre, with a traditional brasserie and bar being the heart and soul of the company's philosophy. Great food, great style, great value, with décor high on the agenda; the bedrooms approach and even in some ways surpass the comforts of home; and everything is at an affordable price.

The food is first class, with a passion for flavour and quality, yet uncomplicated. A range of wholesome traditional dishes made from the best ingredients are married to a list

of eclectic wines, collected and presented by the renowned sommelier Johnny Walker. All prepared and served in an unfussy, unpretentious manner where customers are free to relax and enjoy.

Stunning buildings, striking, contemporary décor and great, unfussy food are only a part of the story: Malmaison's clientele is also looking for consistently excellent customer service. And the secret of being able to deliver on that promise is to employ great people, and then allow them to be themselves. It's a fine balance: service has to be correct, without being over familiar on the one hand or overwhelmingly formal on the other, and there will always be a certain sense of humour (without descending to cheekiness) in a Mal.

There are things that you won't find in a Malmaison: chocolate on the pillow, sheets turned down at night, silver cutlery – but it's by dispensing with such frankly unnecessary frills that Malmaison can afford to deliver such a high quality yet individual service at such a competitive price.

It's a simple vision: but, as with any simple vision, it's delivering on the promise, day in, day out, all year round, that is the true measure of quality. And, ten years after the first two Malmaison hotels opened, in Edinburgh and Glasgow, the group's army of loyal customers stands witness to its success, a fan base rather than a data base, who see Malmaison as an extension of their lifestyle, providing them with the simple things done well with care, consistency and passion in abundance.

malmaison.com

MUSIC TELEVISION®

The pop culture pioneer, MTV provides viewers with intimate access to the music, stars, movies and lifestyles they love. It was the first television channel of its kind anywhere in the world – and despite a host of imitators, it is still first choice for music fans around the globe.

The UK music TV market is possibly the most congested and competitive on the planet. Viewers can choose from 26 music channels specialising in every kind of music in existence. Nine of these channels are operated by MTV: flagship destinations MTV UK & Ireland, VH1 and TMF, plus the music genre-dedicated channels MTV2, MTV Base, MTV Hits, MTV Dance, VH1 Classic and VH2. In 2003, MTV Networks UK won 57% of music viewing with 18.2 million people tuning in each month.

The key to MTV's longevity is both its lack of complacency – it consistently explores the cutting-edge of TV – and its dedication to 'firsts', whether they be the first to show a new video, to talk to an elusive artist or to give viewers the chance to experience the brand in a new, unexpected way.

Crucially, MTV is not just a global network, but a set of proudly local channels, too. MTV UK is unmistakeably British, with a cheeky, irreverent tone and a raft of home-grown hit shows including 'Total Request Live' (TRL), 'Dirty Sanchez', 'Blag' and 'Breaking Point'.

Any TV channel is only as good its relationship with its audience, and MTV strives for viewers to experience it first hand. Recently, MTV2 took

flagship show 'Gonzo' on the road with fifteen new bands. 'Gonzo On Tour' gave viewers the chance to see these emerging acts before anyone else – and to mosh with the MTV2 crew in intimate local venues.

Similarly, when the big, global guns come to town, as per last year's MTV Europe Music Awards hosted by Christina Aguilera in Edinburgh, there is always a regional slant. 7,000 local residents were treated to a free, live simultaneous event and up-and-coming Scottish bands were given an invaluable platform to showcase their talents in 'Breakout Week'. With branding all over Edinburgh (and beyond), more than ever before the awards became an experience and not merely a televised ceremony.

MTV's relationship with the stars is genuinely unrivalled and is evident at every level, from the big names it books, to its marketing and scheduling. Its broadcasts of live gigs feel all the more real due to co-promotion alongside the record labels. MTV broadcast Radiohead's Shepherd's Bush Empire gig live on the eve of their 'Hail To The Thief' album release, and the broadcasts' marketing bore the badge of authenticity with the genuine album artwork.

MTV continually strives to surprise, inspire and innovate… and it's not all just about TV either. MTV now pops up in the classroom and bedroom too. 2004 has seen the launch of 'Boom!', a co-venture with Adobe that sees both brands go into schools to teach kids how to make music videos as part of the national curriculum. MTV has also branched into condoms through a partnership with manufacturer Condomi. This venture (profits from which are channelled into MTV's pro-HIV/AIDS awareness charity 'Staying Alive') is designed to reduce the stigma of buying condoms with embarrassment-free innovative 'MTV' packaging, thus making it easier for young adults to ensure their sex is safe.

Combining relevant UK programming, audacious local initiatives and smash US hits like 'The Osbournes', 'Punk'd' and 'Cribs', it's no wonder that MTV still reigns supreme.

mtv.co.uk

NOKIA
CONNECTING PEOPLE

If you've got a mobile phone in your pocket or sitting on your desk right now the chances are it's a Nokia: more than one in three mobile phones sold globally is a Nokia phone.

Nokia's vision is Connecting People – to other people, and to their passions. The growth of mobile communication has made it possible for everyone to stay in touch with the people that matter to them and the information which they find important. Nokia develops mobile devices that support everyone's lifestyle – whether they are a fashionista, an active type, a business professional or a serious mobile gamer. The brand is dedicated to enhancing people's lives and productivity by providing easy-to-use, secure products and solutions for imaging, games, media, mobile network operators and businesses.

Nokia is a high tech company with an unusual history. It was founded in 1865 by mining engineer Fredrik Idestam. Initially the company manufactured paper and card then moved onto rubber. In the 1920s, Nokia took over the Finnish Cable Works in Helsinki, which saw the start of an industrial conglomerate that survived until the 1990s, with the company making anything from rubber tyres and cables to boats and raincoats.

In the 1980s, Nokia began manufacturing mobile phones. The Mobira Talkman was the world's first transportable phone (complete with a 22lb charging box the size of a suitcase) and in 1987 it launched the Cityman (which at the time was compared to the size of a brick), the first hand-held mobile phone. Since the 1990s, Nokia has focused on mobile communications and, through a clever mix of technology and aesthetics, has become the world leader in mobile communications.

Since the Mobira Talkman, Nokia has continued to be a technology trailblazer. Nokia handsets were the first to feature text messaging, to access internet-based information services and to have integrated cameras. Now Nokia is leading the charge to the third generation

Easy, reliable, stylish and cool

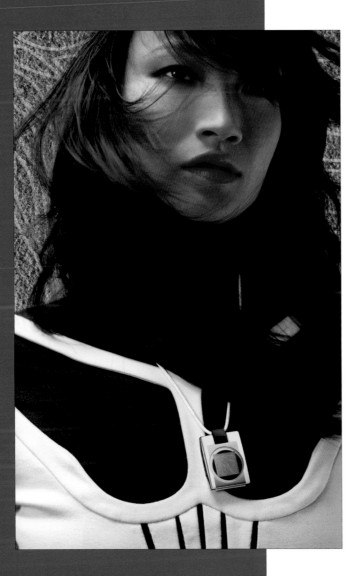

of mobile telephony in which mobile communications, information technology and media industries will converge, as well as diversifying into mobile gaming with the launch of N-Gage.

Design is a fundamental building block of the Nokia brand. Less than a decade ago, all mobile phones seemed to be black. Then Nokia introduced colour to its products and everything changed. The mobile phone suddenly became a statement of personal style, communicating more about the owner's identity than any electronic product before.

Nokia was the first company to introduce changeable covers, enabling people to personalise the look of their phone in seconds. Continuing to pioneer new forms of personalisation and communication, Nokia has introduced ring tones, graphics, downloadable applications, text messaging and multimedia devices. But at the heart of Nokia design is usability: product's interfaces are easy to navigate, displays are large enough for the task in hand, keypads are pleasant to the touch and the size and shape is comfortable and appropriate.

Nokia's enduring success is not just down to its products – savvy marketing has also played a role. Recognising mobile phones were a fashion accessory, Nokia was one of the first technology brands to pin its colours to the fashion industry, sponsoring London Fashion Week since 1999.

In the youth arena, Nokia is heavily involved in lifestyle sports events, including the FIS Snowboarding World Cup and the Rip Curl Newquay Boardmasters surf festival, and runs its own annual urban sports and music event, Totally Board.

Music and the concept of mobile music is a new departure for Nokia this year; its latest venture is to help resurrect the Isle of Wight Festival, which this year attracted the likes of David Bowie and the Manic Street Preachers.

nokia.co.uk

O₂

In a competitive market, it is important to always remain focused on the customer. O₂'s core strategy is customer-centricity – putting the customer first and delivering products and services based upon their needs.

O₂ was officially launched on May 1st 2002, following the demerger of mmO2 from BT the previous November, but in only two years it has already achieved enormous brand recognition, despite spending relatively little on advertising compared with its bigger rivals. At launch in May 2002, it began its high-profile brand building campaign, using the visually striking image of oxygen bubbles in blue water that has become its trademark symbol. By the end of the launch phase, which involved advertising across TV, print and poster media, supported by direct marketing, O₂ had become a well-known brand, achieving levels of recognition on a par with its longer established rivals.

The key to its success is its focused approach to product and service development and to marketing, concentrating on customer insight and executing campaigns that engage customers in an exciting and fresh way.

Although voice services are still what mobile handsets are mainly used for, customers are increasingly interested in mobile data services. First, it was simple messages: but now it's more innovative applications, such as media messaging (MMS), mobile games and video services. 3G services is another area of future growth, although O₂ takes a cautious and measured approach, and will only launch such services when technology, handsets and the customers are all ready.

O₂ is developing a range of innovative data solutions, such as Europe's first mobile device to download high quality music. The Digital Music Player, launched in November 2003, was described by Stuff magazine as "Conceptually the most exciting thing we've seen" while The Independent called it "A neat and efficient way of having the music you want to listen to, without waiting to get home to your computer".

O₂ is also adept at customising products to fit the needs and interests of its different user groups. For example, 41% of the key youth market does not have access to a landline (Source: Sweeney Pinedo Q2 03/04) while those that do often use a mobile in lieu. So O_2 pioneered technology that allows it to launch O_2 Home, the only Pay & Go to offer lower cost mobile calls from home.

In its marketing, O_2 tries to be as relevant to its users as possible – for example, its sponsorship deals actually stimulate immediate use of its products, rather than only building brand awareness. Take the range of text alerts, sports-related news updates and interactive quizzes that O_2 developed to complement its partnerships with Arsenal Football Club and the England Rugby Squad. Or the partnership with Big Brother, the biggest, most interactive media property on UK television, providing the ideal vehicle to drive brand awareness and demonstrate O_2 products such as media messaging and video alerts.

O_2 also has a strong commitment to corporate responsibility, and features in several of the main sustainability indices and funds, such as the Dow Jones Sustainability Indexes, the FTSE4Good Index Series, and the new UK Business in the Community Corporate Responsibility Index.

O_2 is bold, full of surprises, continually coming up with ideas that are practical and relevant, opening up a world of exciting possibilities. Yet it is clear and straightforward, and can turn highly complex technology into products that are easy to understand and use. It listens to people and is open and candid, and so is trusted by its customers. Above all else, O_2 is a brand that makes things possible – a brand with a 'can do' attitude to life.

Music through your mobile. Whenever. Wherever.

Digital Music Player.

o2.co.uk/music

O_2

o2.co.uk

orange™

Orange is the UK's most popular mobile phone network, and one of Europe's leading telecommunications companies. In Britain, it has more than 13.6 million active customers, while across the world, 49 million people use its services. It is number one in most of the countries where it operates. Not bad for a brand only celebrating its tenth birthday (in April 2004).

What set Orange apart from the outset was the clarity of its communications. In 1994, the UK mobile phone market was confusing, complicated and expensive. So Orange began building a strong, fresh, clear identity that cut through the clutter, the high-tech jargon and the complicated pricing plans. It was revolutionary.

Orange knew from the start that the way to stay ahead of the pack was by providing the best and most innovative service to its customers, and numerous awards for customer satisfaction – such as the J D Power and Associates UK Mobile Customer Satisfaction Study – prove that it can deliver.

Orange was the first mobile phone brand to offer customer-friendly innovations such as simple Talk Plans that offered real value for money, per second billing, Caller ID, itemised billing free of charge, and direct customer relationships. And Orange has continued to innovate over the past decade, launching the world's first Microsoft Windows powered smartphone, the Orange SPV and personal phone trainers, who help customers make the most of their Orange phones.

During 2004, Orange has been busy adding two compelling business offerings, both European firsts. Talk Now is a 'Push to Talk' service, allowing multi-person conference calls to be set up at the push of a single button, while the Orange M2M Connect platform makes it easy to set up machine-to-machine communications solutions via its combined network and data platform. That means, for example, that a vending machine will be able to order up supplies for itself when it's running low, without the need for a site visit by an employee, so offering improved customer service and lower costs.

As the world of mobile communications inevitably merges with that of entertainment and the media, so Orange continues to develop relationships with books, film and music.

Orange's links with the film industry include: its witty 'Orange Film Commission' advertising reminding cinemagoers to turn off their mobile phones; it also sponsors the Belfast Film Festival; the Orange Wednesday partnership with the Cinema Marketing Association, which allows Orange customers to take a friend to a film for free every Wednesday; the Orange Word season of talks by leading screenwriters; and the Orange Pitch competition, with a prize of £1000 and script development training.

In the world of books, the brand is present through the Orange Prize for Fiction (the only UK book award celebrating women's fiction), the Orange Award for New Writers and the Orange Labyrinth online community for creative writing.

Orange sponsors 'music 247' tents at musical festivals up and down the UK, including Glastonbury, The Carling Weekend (Reading and Leeds) and T in the Park. Music lovers can get the latest festival news and free text alerts sent to their mobiles, to keep them in touch with what's happening wherever they are.

Orange is also a global citizen, and to celebrate the brand's tenth birthday, employees from around the world are taking part in a charity event dubbed 'One Orange'. Inspired by the way the Olympic Torch travels from country to country, staff will walk, sail, row, cycle, glide, skate-board – indeed, use any mode of transport that does not involve a motor – the total distance between all countries in the Orange group. Proceeds from these fundraising activities will go to UNICEF.

In 1948, Rudolf Dassler founded PUMA from the remains of his family's shoe business in Herzogenaurach, Germany. The early decades were very much about sport, about running shoes and football boots featuring the now globally recognised 'form stripe', about Olympic champions from Tommy Smith to Heike Dreschler, and about football legends from Pele to Maradona.

Through the 1970s, the leaping Cat logo of the basketball and tennis ranges became synonymous with urban cool, immediately identifying its wearer as an individual with a particular attitude about both life and sport.

In the 1980s, however, as the global sportswear market began to accelerate and transform itself into a world of hyper-marketing, massive athlete endorsement contracts and 'logo-as-design', the brand went through a process of re-organisation. Every player in the marketplace was competing to be exactly the same as everyone else, so PUMA asked itself the key question: "Yes, we're a sports brand, but what else?"

PUMA had to become more than it had been in its past. After taking a close look at what the brand had been good at, examining the changing marketplace, and looking closely at the attitudes of its core consumers, it became clear that PUMA was far from what might be considered a traditional sportswear company.

For years, the brand had delivered a dual proposition – performance as well as lifestyle. Taking the lead from its own audience, listening to what consumers were saying with their behaviour, the brand defined itself in both ways, and began to 'mix things up'. No individual is one-dimensional, interested in only sport or only fashion. It was therefore concluded that PUMA's brand personality should likewise never be limited. The definition of a new category, 'sportlifestyle' was born.

However, this transition was not an easy undertaking. For years, growth was slow, and challenges were numerous. But, as an understanding of 'mixing it up' developed within the company, things began to click. By the late 1990s,

the comeback was fully underway, typified by new ways of thinking about PUMA and the marketplace – partnerships with musicians and artists, the return of heritage shoe styles, development of sport-fashion collections – all were PUMA firsts.

As market share grew and the logo began to reappear as an underground alternative to the typical offerings of an overheated sports market, things began to really take off – new advertising, new websites, new retail stores in key cities around the globe, and a new understanding of the way consumers react to the brand.

The leaping Cat became an icon of the underground – a symbol for the 'alternative' to the norm.

'Mixing things up' continues to drive the brand into new territory. Latest innovations include a partnership with the Jamaican Olympic team resulting in a collection of sport-inspired lifestyle apparel as well as unique explorations into the worlds of Jamaican music and culture. PUMA's co-operation with Juergen Teller on the recent 'Hello' campaign has delivered a distinct brand message reflecting the brand's ebullience, love of life and positive energy. Meanwhile, concentration on growth in the retail business has positioned the brand to deliver a pure brand message to consumers around the world. Crucially, maintaining a strong focus on product design has resulted in innumerable distinctive pieces of apparel, footwear, and accessories that have garnered attention in the fashion and design press.

Building on a long heritage of originality and continuing a strong concentration on the goal of providing distinctive and unique products has allowed PUMA to move comfortably into its new role as a design innovator and market leader. As for the future – well, you can count on exciting developments from this groundbreaking brand.

STICK STICK STICK ✉
Proud Sponsor of the **Jamaican Relay Team**

puma.com

RICHARD JAMES
SAVILE ROW

> Where classic British tailoring and the 21st century design aesthetic collide

Signature sharp lines and sleek silhouettes are the hallmark of leading British menswear label Richard James, reflecting its commitment to a fusion of the classic and the contemporary, a true 21st century interpretation of the traditional Savile Row look.

Exclusive fabrics, strong design direction and the highest quality manufacturing has attracted a large and varied clientele: Sir Paul McCartney married Heather Mills wearing a bespoke Richard James suit, shirt and tie, while Tom Cruise, Liam Gallagher, Hugh Grant, Jarvis Cocker, Usher and Sir Elton John are also customers. Nor is the Richard James' appeal restricted to men: Annie Lennox, Madonna and Nicole Kidman are fans, too.

The label has attracted a slew of awards as well, including the London Evening Standard's Retailer of the Year in 1997 and both the British Fashion Council's Menswear Designer of the Year and GQ magazine's Designer of the Year in 2001. Not bad for a label which is barely twelve years old.

Established in 1992 by Richard James and Sean Dixon, the label's designs are cutting edge, with heavy use of unusual and unconventional fabrics in strikingly modern patterns and colours – as when Robert De Niro and Dustin Hoffman were featured on the cover of US magazine George in Richard James camouflage suits. Yet at the same time, the collection draws heavily on Britain's past, with suits featuring body-conscious nipped-in waists, flared cuffs and double vents. As Richard James himself says: "It is almost a caricature of the traditional British look classic but special clothes that are not boring or 'dusty'."

In its flagship Savile Row store (the largest retail space on what is arguably the world's most prestigious street for menswear) and its premises in the City of London's luxury emporium, The Royal Exchange, the vibrant colour combinations and superb fabrics and prints which characterise the Richard James collection are perfectly set off by polished beech wood floors, white walls and light and airy space.

In addition to the Savile Row and Mayfair collections of suits, overcoats, jackets and even cardigans (but all with that Richard James' stylish twist), evening wear, an extensive range of shirts and pure silk ties and the Savile Sport casual clothing line, the shops also display the label's other products. These include the accessories (wallets, credit card holders and belts), English hand-made shoes, cufflinks in sculpted silver, colour-shot glass or precious stones, as well as Richard James fragrances and grooming products. Complementing the off-the-peg clothing ranges, clients can opt for the label's bespoke, British-made tailoring service, or, for the more casual look, there is the limited edition luxury jean and jean jacket range, trimmed with customised buttons and rivets.

Over the years, the success of the London stores has created enormous demand from other prestigious retail outlets, and now the collection can be found in Selfridges, Harvey Nichols and Liberty in the UK, Colette in Paris, David Jones in Australia, Lane Crawford in Asia and Saks, Barney's and Bergdorf Goodman in the US.

Grounded in English tailoring tradition Richard James may be: but the label's constant reinvention of what tradition is keeps it relevant to new generations of customers in a way that should keep Savile Row at the heart of the fashion universe for years to come.

richardjames.co.uk

RIZLA+.

Colourful, down to earth and inspirational

Sold in over 120 countries, Rizla is the world's leading manufacturer and supplier of rolling papers. It is the original rolling paper, with a rich heritage to match.

Pierre de Lacroix, founder of the family business that went on to define the roll-your-own papers market over the following four centuries, began making paper in 1532. In 1660, the Lacroix family began producing rolling papers for tobacco in the Dordogne, and by 1850 the manufacture of rolling papers as a mass-market product was finally perfected.

The Rizla brand name was first registered – as Riz-La+. – in 1866, and is derived from 'riz', referring to the rice-paper used at the time, and 'la+.', an enigmatic abbreviation of the Lacroix family name. In 1954, the brand lost its gap and became Rizla+. which it has been ever since. The next landmark for Rizla came in 1997 when it was acquired by Imperial Tobacco.

With over three quarters of UK roll-your-own smokers choosing to use Rizla papers, the brand is truly synonymous with the rolling papers category. Total sales are in excess of 330 million booklets per year.

Rizla advertising focuses on powerful and visually arresting images where the pack takes an animated role. Everyday consumer language and banter is used in all marketing communications.

Rizla recognises the high penetration of paper users interested in motorbikes with its Rizla Suzuki British Superbikes Team. With British Superbikes being fast paced, colourful and accessible it matches perfectly with the Rizla brand.

KING SIZE SLIM

RIZLA +

SLIM

QUALITY PAPERS

FINEST QUALITY GUMMED PAPERS

The Rizla Café has formed a major part of the PR campaign for a number of years. Providing a warm, clean and comfortable haven in environments that are often cold and wet, such as the Glastonbury festival, Rizla was pioneering in this imaginative form of communication that has since been followed by other brands. Consumers can interact with the brand and be entertained by cutting edge DJs, whilst lounging on Rizla Rolling Sofas. Rizlaware, the brand's clothing range which fuses function with fashion, is sold in the Rizla Café enabling consumers to take a piece of the brand away with them.

Rizlaware is also sold on Rizla.co.uk, the brand's website, which welcomes consumers into the world of Rizla and is informative as well as entertaining, offering information on products and the differences between them as well as an arcade section full of games which have been 'Rizlarised'.

The launch of Rizla KS Slim Silver illustrates the brand's leading edge position in the rolling papers category. Rizla KS Slim Silver is an ultra thin paper, so allowing the full flavour of the tobacco to be appreciated. This premium product has watermarked papers and quality packaging. The launch, towards the end of 2003, was supported through all communication channels, including outdoor and press advertising, the painting of the Rizla Suzuki British Superbikes Team silver, a unique direct mail campaign, and a designer collaboration with Mrs Jones to produce exclusive Rizla Silver clothing items.

This year Rizla will unveil a major new creative proposition, based around the theme of Inspiration. Rizla's 'Inspired By' campaign will explore the processes through which we expand our frontiers and create new boundaries, celebrating iconic inspirational figures, past, present and future. The proposition will be supported with an exciting new visual identity featuring the iconic Rizla cross, as well as a national events programme across six UK cities, where the brand will facilitate a series of live performances, exhibitions and workshops from influential and inspirational musical talent.

Rizla is a brand full of heritage which continues to lead the rolling papers category through innovation and communication.

rizla.co.uk

RUBY & MILLIE

Ruby and Millie, the self-confessed make-up obsessives who developed this brand, each have a wealth of expert knowledge and experience behind them. Indeed, it was highly inevitable that Ruby, a world renowned make-up artist who has created looks for the world's top photographers and most influential fashion designers – including John Galliano, Jasper Conran and Ghost – would have her own cosmetics line one day. It was more than fortunate that Millie, an internationally successful beauty publicist who has worked with brands like Aveda and Shu Uemura, should market the concept.

The two partners were originally approached by Boots to work on a beauty project which developed into the Ruby & Millie brand. After two years of development, the brand was unveiled in the UK in 1998 using Harvey Nichols department stores in London and Leeds as the launch pad. It was subsequently rolled out at larger Boots stores nationwide.

Ruby & Millie proved to be immensely popular, which led to the brand facing rapid expansion, with the cosmetics range now in over 100 stores nationwide. The year 2000 saw the publication of 'Face Up', Ruby & Millie's first beauty book, which coincided with the launch of their accessories range, now available in almost 600 stores.

Ruby & Millie is exclusive to Boots and has been hailed as one of the most innovative brands to be launched in the international beauty sector for decades. It brings together the experience of two beauty industry

professionals, Ruby Hammer and Millie Kendal who, over a period of two years, lovingly created a range of almost 300 products. Each item has been approved by both women, to form a collection that Ruby and Millie are happy to wear themselves; perhaps more importantly, they are confident that their friends, mothers, grandmothers and children would want to wear Ruby & Millie, too.

The Ruby & Millie philosophy is to create beauty that is achievable and affordable, enabling all women to accentuate their natural beauty and feel glamorous and gorgeous.

It is sophisticated yet simple; experimental yet accessible; and above all, fun. These values extend throughout the brand. Its packaging, co-designed by Wright & Teague, has been developed using a combination of mirrored and transparent materials to echo the individual's identity while reflecting the brand's integrity. It has been imitated by many mainstream brands, and has become a stable entity in the application and design of modern cosmetics.

Another key element of the brand is the environment in which it is sold. Its in-store boutiques were designed by Hosker, Moore & Kent with the aim of being a playground for women to have fun and experiment. Hard sell techniques and complex makeovers are abandoned in favour of the concept of an in-store Make-up Advisor. The idea here is to provide friendly advice that women really want, with solutions to their specific problems. The advisors treat the work area as if it were a dressing table, and use the mirror to show customers how to apply their make-up, with their own faces serving as canvases for experimentation.

As Ruby and Millie have said, "Ruby & Millie is for the individual who aspires to being strong yet demure, professional yet sexy, young yet mature. It's all about the freedom to choose who you want to be today."

rubyandmillie.com

Sporty, distinctive cars for
discerning individuals

Conceived by aeronautical engineers, the first generation of Saab cars rolled off the production line in Sweden half a century ago. Unrestricted by conventional automotive design wisdom, the early cars marked the beginning of a distinctive theme that was to characterise a brand.

In today's market, Saab's individuality has stood it in good stead against rival brands and reinforces its position as the 'alternative' premium manufacturer. With a comprehensive product line-up embracing sporting saloon, estate and one of the best selling convertible models, Saab has established itself as a significant player in the sector.

The bold lines of a Saab readily set the car apart from others on the road. Contemporary, sleek styling combined with lateral design has created a distinct and inspirational look and feel that has been the foundation of the brand for over 50 years – in sync with the cosmopolitan and individualistic nature of the Saab driver.

Saab's unique approach to design is more than just skin deep, as the originality and flair on the outside is coupled with excellent performance and driver safety within. By designing the vehicle around the driver, engineers have created a range that is as practical as it is stylish. You can tell that Saab has listened to its market and created cars that suit its demanding, diverse lifestyles.

Take the latest incarnation of the 9-3 convertible for example. From the outset, it was developed with the belief that an open top car should be 'more than a convertible'. The car has retained Saab's sporty and fun to drive characteristics and includes a plethora of innovative product features, making it the ultimate car for all seasons.

Saab has always wanted its customers to enjoy driving and engine performance is paramount. Saab's reputation founded on its expertise in turbo-charging technology – it was the first manufacturer to put a turbo-charged car into volume production. A Saab turbo-charged engine generates smooth pulling power at any engine speed, ensuring overtaking is swift and controlled. It is surprising then to discover that, compared to its competitors, all Saab cars offer more power and performance per £.

Motoring pleasure also manifests itself in the comfort of the interior. More than 30 years ago, models were already being fitted with heated front seats; and today the award winning design and comfort of Saab's seats is an industry benchmark. Add to this the fact that Saab cars are among the safest on the road and drivers can be reassured that they are protected by a host of high tech features, including the world's first interactive head restraints.

So, in terms of technological advances, Saab has been quietly ahead of the game for many years. In 1991, it became the only UK automobile manufacturer to equip all models with anti-lock brakes as standard and has been fitting side impact bars and energy absorbing bumpers to all its models since 1972. More recent advances include the introduction of direct ignition and on-board engine software, which is more powerful than that used in the Apollo space capsules that put man on the moon.

Saab takes pride in its individual way of thinking and, in a continuous effort to avoid the mainstream, its refined and sophisticated marketing takes a refreshing move away from the techniques adopted by many of the other premium carmakers. Key elements that incorporate the brand values of originality, innovation, style, performance and safety are consistently communicated to reaffirm the Saab's integrity and distinguish it from its premium competitors.

With its evolutionary product development strategy, Saab continues to progress its vehicle range in response to the changing and developing needs of its customers and is increasingly becoming the manufacturer of choice for individuals leading active, sporting lives.

saab.co.uk

sass & bide

What is sass & bide? To paraphrase a great poet, 'it is easier to catch the wind than it is to describe your beauty….'

sass & bide is so difficult to define in words, yet it is instantly recognisable to its many fans around the world. It has been described as a love of all things creative, a passion for individuality and freedom of expression, and the intuitive fusion of contradictory elements to form a beautiful whole.

Perhaps, more than anything else, the sass & bide philosophy is encapsulated by the realisation of a dream shared by best friends Sarah-Jane Clarke and Heidi Middleton – a dream that has been realised by an unwavering pursuit to remain true to your own path no matter what.

It all began in London's famed vintage stores, and on the streets of its eclectic markets, indulging their obsession with fashion during moments stolen from their 'real' jobs. Their first foray into fashion started with innovative denim jeans sold at a market stall in London's Portobello Road, and provided the first taste of what was to come.

sass & bide, as they have always known each other, achieved an instant hit in the notoriously competitive market with their unique denim creations. Utilising Heidi's life long passion for innovative design, and Sarah-Jane's extraordinary sense of style in bringing the pieces together to create a total look, the girls were facing increasing

numbers of enthusiastic repeat customers and referrals every weekend. The dream they had shared since before they even met, of launching their own fashion label, was on the verge of becoming real.

In 1999 the girls decided to return to Australia, settling in Sydney to launch their namesake label, and focus on revolutionising the designer denim market. The sense of unaffected glamour, confident sexiness and the use of contradiction that defines their own sense of style, provided the inspiration for the incredibly successful east village jean. An international following soon developed, and the passion of their fans gave the girls both their greatest sense of satisfaction, and a powerful validation of their desire to take sass & bide in bold new directions.

In 2001, with the support of Mercedes Australian Fashion Week in Sydney, Australia, sass & bide launched their first seasonal fashion collection, 'Lady Punk'. The collection was received to rave reviews, both in the domestic and the international press. The sass & bide fashion line was created, and now comprises four trans-seasonal collections a year. Since 2003 sass & bide has showcased on the international fashion arena through the highly successful shows at London Fashion Week and in February 2004 during New York Fashion Week, expanding the label's runway presence and driving the sass & bide vision for the future.

Today sass & bide is sold in some of the best boutiques and department stores around the world, and enjoys the enviable support of both the fashion press, and the 'it' girls we read about in their pages every month. However, it is the girl on the street, and the impact sass & bide has had on her, that provides the inspiration to continue to push the boundaries, to defy the limits of convention, and to continue to live the dream shared by Sarah-Jane Clarke and Heidi Middleton.

Heidi Middleton first wrote these words of Emily Bronte in her diary as a fourteen year old, and it's a message that resonates with sass & bide today more than ever – 'I'll walk where my own nature leads me. It vexes me to choose another guide.'

sassandbide.com

SELFRIDGES&C͎

An innovative and inspiring space, continuously challenging the concepts of retail.

The inspiring space that is Selfridges began with Gordon Selfridge, the US entrepreneur who founded the store in London's Oxford Street in 1909. For Selfridge, the department store lay at the heart of urban life and, because of this, it was imperative it brought its theatre and passion to all.

In keeping with his beliefs, the Selfridges of 2004 has sought to deliver inspiration and creativity to all of its customers. Having opened its iconic Birmingham site, designed by the acclaimed architects Future Systems, in 2003, Selfridges is now made up of four stores, all offering different interpretations of the retail experience. Culture is at the heart of the Selfridges brand. Collaborating with artists ensures concepts remain original and fresh throughout the whole Selfridges identity.

Selfridges' relationship with the arts has flourished since Sam Taylor-Wood's work, XV Seconds, wrapped the Oxford Street store in 2000 with the world's largest photographic artwork. This relationship continues, and the in-house marketing team have recently worked with a number of artists such as Barbara Kruger, Alison Jackson and Rankin.

Selfridges has also forged creative partnerships with galleries including The Serpentine, The Victoria and Albert Museum and the Icon Gallery.

Last year, this connection with the arts was taken to unprecedented lengths with Body Craze. An event celebrating the body in all its diversity, the launch of Body Craze witnessed a Spencer Tunick installation featuring six hundred naked bodies. Artists showcased throughout the event included (amongst many others) Random Dance,

John Kamikaze, the amazing Acrobat Production artists and the award-winning dance theatre company, Frantic Assembly.

In November 2003 Selfridges launched Superbrands in its London store, pioneering a new concept in designerwear retailing. Featuring eight of today's most influential and exceptional designers, Superbrands is a shopping revolution. Designed by the architect David Adjaye, a red resin tunnel leads through to a room that features a pixilated sky showing the contrast between night and day. At the heart of designer brands such as Dolce and Gabbana, Balenciaga and Marni sits Momo, one of the most renowned restaurants in London. The clash and contrast between the minimal aesthetic appearance of the Superbrand in the room and the ethnic chic of Momo is classic Selfridges.

The most recent of Selfridges cultural events was Brasil 40°. Described as an explosion of Brasilian culture, the promotion celebrated some of Brasil's most accomplished musicians, dancers, film-makers, designers, artists and photographers. The front of the Oxford Street store was transformed into the skyline of Rio de Janeiro with a 13m replica of the statue of Christ the Redeemer, designed by Abel Gomes, taking centre-stage. Selfridges also worked with a number of high profile artists and performers including Mario Testino, Fernando Meirelles (City of God director), the famous furniture designers Campana Brothers, the footballer Denilson, and fashion designer Carlos Meile.

To top it off, Selfridges picked up numerous awards in 2003. These include Drapers Record Store of the Year Award, Glamour Magazine Most Glamorous Department Store Award, In Style Magazine Best London Department Store, Best for Service, Best Beauty Hall, Best Partner and Best to Blow £1000 and, in conjunction with the Bullring, Selfridges Birmingham triumphed with the Retail Destination of the Year Award.

Reinforcing the vision of its founder, Selfridges has spent the last year reinventing the concept of the department store and the shopping experience that happens inside.

selfridges.co.uk

SOMERSET HOUSE

After over 200 years of history as a centre of government, Somerset House opened to the public in the year 2000 as an inspirational setting for world famous collections of art, outdoor performances and elegant eateries. What were once gloomy offices now host a wide range of high-profile public programmes designed to engage Londoners of all ages and all backgrounds, as well as visitors to the city.

The building now embraces the masterpieces of the Courtauld collection – the Manets, the Gauguins and the Renoirs – the exotic treasures from St Petersburg displayed in the Hermitage Rooms and the Gilbert Collection of decorative arts, not to mention Somerset House's dramatic neoclassical façade. All of these treasures now provide a permanent backdrop for the diverse activities in the Courtyard.

As design guru Stephen Bayley comments: "Can there be any more complete a symbol of urban transformation than this former Inland Revenue office, now replaced by the Courtauld Institute with its bright Impressionists and the central courtyard that is now a vast public piazza dedicated to aesthetes, gourmets and (in winter) skaters rather than sadistic tax inspectors?" (The Rebirth of London's Waterside, High Life, June 2003).

The Courtyard, restored to its original 18th century appearance, is reinvented all year round as the capital's grand living room. In spring, summer and autumn, its fountains create a natural children's playground. Summer nights attract crowds for P J Harvey, Goldfrapp, Royksopp, Air, Underworld and a host of other stars. In winter, the courtyard is transformed into an ice rink, while at other times of year it's an open air cinema or simply a space for quiet relaxation.

The River Terrace, with its spectacular views over the Thames, is a new thoroughfare for pedestrians, linking the north and south banks of the river.

Since it opened to the public in 2000, the new Somerset House has attracted over one million visitors a year. Diverse audiences have been drawn by the artistic and historical treasures and by the superb programme of innovative events which make new and exciting use of the space and which interpret the site's historic, architectural, and cultural wealth.

Event-led marketing, strong media relations, and the development of a strong visual identity have communicated the message that Somerset House is the place for a special experience, whether you are going to a gig, visiting a gallery, going ice skating, or having a meal.

Research has shown that media coverage and word-of-mouth recommendation are key sources of information for visitors. Specific marketing and press campaigns are tailored for each event and exhibition, and are supported by an ongoing marketing programme communicating the diversity of things to do and see at Somerset House, and the range of engaging experiences available in this very special environment.

At the heart of Somerset House lies a famous classical building, so it is fitting that the visual identity uses a distinctive element from that building – the arch keystone – to give it distinctiveness among a host of competing arts venues. The keystone is simply the most timeless and enduring representation of all the faces of Somerset House, including the building itself, the activities and events that happen here, and the cultural context it fits within.

It also symbolises the original and innovative vision that is continually reinventing Somerset House for the enjoyment of Londoners and its visitors.

somerset-house.org.uk

Sony Ericsson

Simplicity, design, quality, technical brilliance

Sony Ericsson is the mobile phone joint venture formed by Sony of Japan and Ericsson of Sweden in October 2001. Combining Sony quality and design with Ericsson's position as a world-renowned technical innovator has united two distinct brands into one new, fresh one – therefore 1+1=3.

The mobile phone industry is a highly competitive arena with many large, well known companies striving to be number one, with the goal of being the brand of choice for an increasingly knowledgeable consumer.

When Sony and Ericsson, two diverse and well established brands, combined, the objective was to create a new brand that was fresh, unique and instantly recognisable. A brand that consumers could come to trust, conveying the marriage of the stunning design, functionality and empowerment of one partner with the technical brilliance of the other.

At the start of the joint venture it was vital the brand was established quickly as its competitors include some of the biggest media spenders in the advertising world.

People are defined by the two separate sides of the brain that create their identity, the left being logical and the right creative. This has helped shape the company's personality and product development strategy. On the left side it has logic, which is focused on simplicity of design, connectivity and ease of use, while the right side is creative, which drives the amazing applications that create the sense of wonder and magic. Together they define Sony Ericsson as an extension of oneself – 'another me'.

It is a simple idea with great implications. Consumers, in combination with their Sony Ericsson device, create a greater, more enabled individual. It's a partnership of personalities, shared, infused, together.

Everything Sony Ericsson produces in the way of product must portray the brand's identity. Sony Ericsson's products are at the forefront of this communication, as it is the most interactive experience between consumers and the brand. Simultaneously, everything that the brand produces must illustrate the aspects of 'simplicity'. This includes all corporate and product based literature, advertising, public relations materials, point-of-sale materials – everything.

It is the aim of Sony Ericsson to create communications products with great applications and content focusing on imaging, gaming, music and connectivity. The products should also be trendsetting, easy to use and simple to personalise. Sony Ericsson is driven by product, from which brand experiences grow. The Product is always the hero.

Sony Ericsson products bear the hallmarks of the brand promise. The T610, T630, Z600, K700 and S700 which are all strong in design, rich in features and lead the imaging market, but they have a quality that make them stand out from the crowd.

This ease of use and simplicity is brought to market by such concepts as QuickShare™ – officially the easiest way to send and share pictures. QuickShare™ allows people to take pictures with the fewest amount of 'clicks' on their phones. This is unrivalled in the market today – and this is all part of the Sony Ericsson design philosophy and brand promise.

The brand focuses on the matra 'We must make our own path, stand out and be unique'. This is Sony Ericsson.

sonyericcson.com/uk

sophia kokosalaki

Contemporary, original, labour-intensive, directional, timeless

Sophia Kokosalaki, the Athens-born, London-based designer, is the unlikely outsider who now has the most important show in London Fashion Week's calendar. Arriving in London in 1996 after studying Greek and English literature at the University of Athens, she enrolled on the MA in Womenswear at Central St Martin's college of Art and Design.

Her graduate show in 1998 made it to the window of South Molton Street's Pellicano. Similar exposure in the window of Browns, another South Molton Street boutique, had launched the careers of John Galliano and Hussein Chalayan.

Sophia's clothes are a great balancing act between fragile beauty and assertiveness, maintaining femininity and toughness in equal measure. As the designer herself says, she likes to "create tension between the romantic and the dynamic".

In a similar way, she also manages to balance cleverly the underground and the commercial. Her distinctive design identity, based loosely on references from her Greek roots, features classical draping moving unexpectedly across the body, precise tailoring, inventive knitwear and use of traditional handcraft techniques such as cording, crochet webbing and macramé. However complicated it may sound, though, the outcome is resolutely modern and wearable. Her clothes do not compromise the wearer and, however intricate they may be in terms of construction and technique, they look thoroughly effortless and glamorously cool once on.

Among Kokosalaki's achievements are the reinvention of the black dress – modernising it with distinctive details and unexpected mixes of materials such as leather with jersey and tulle – and her inventive treatment of leather, with new techniques introduced with each collection. Indeed, her unique approach to using of leather, treating it more like fabric than a tough material, led to her appointment at Ruffo Research, the Milanese leather house, where she was a designer for two seasons, encouraged by them to create a fresh, more experimental line of leatherwear for men and women. There Sophia gained

international exposure. By the end of her stint at Ruffo, she had become one of the few names that had the pulling power to bring in the international press and buyers in London for her immensely sleek catwalk presentations.

Kokosalaki's clothes are aimed at free-minded individuals who are looking to create a distinctive look without wearing anything that is loud or overtly sexy and attention seeking. Not one to follow the trends that dominate a season, but rather wanting to create them and give directions for others to follow, she has acquired a loyal customer base who know and love her intricate technique. Those who mostly covet her collections are fashion insiders who admire the evolution of the elements that make a Kokosalaki piece so unique, particularly her sensitivity in the use of tradition, applied to bring out a thoroughly modern result that has no references to the past.

At a time when most designers use directly obvious elements of the 1950s, 1960s, 1970s and 1980s in their collection, Sophia carefully uses the most discreet details to create clothes that are contemporary yet timeless. Her originality of design has been recognised by the British Art Foundation, which awarded her with the first Fellowship for Fashion.

Not one to embrace the overt use of celebrity endorsement, she is mostly known through the quiet revolution of her work and championed by the fashion cognoscenti who last year awarded her with the Best New Generation Designer award at the British Style Awards.

Among her current projects are an expansion of her line to include accessories, as well as plans to broaden her small line of shoes to a full collection of footwear.

More importantly, this summer she will unveil her costumes for the Opening and Closing Ceremonies at the Athens Olympic Games.

sophiakokosalaki.com

STA TRAVEL

EXPERIENCE IS EVERYTHING

A passion for travel;
a desire to be different

In 1975, an intrepid bunch of Australian travellers fresh off the hippy trail decided to establish a different sort of travel company.

Their idea was simple: to move away from the traditional high street travel agencies, with their emphasis on package holidays, and instead do something completely new. Their ambition was to start a company that specialised in serving those who had largely been ignored by the travel industry: independent travellers and the student market. They also wanted a company that stood apart from its rivals: that was young, fresh, adventurous and attracted those with an enduring passion for travel and a free-spirited, intrepid attitude. In other words, a company that would appeal to people like themselves. And so, from these rather small beginnings on a university campus down under, STA Travel was born.

It's now 25 years since the first UK office opened, but the same attitude still pervades STA Travel today. Step into any of its 65 UK branches and you can be sure that the consultants will be young (the average age is mid 20s), helpful and well travelled. While other agencies fill their offices with uniformed employees, STA Travel fills its with informed ones, who are head-over-heels in love with travelling, have experience of what it is all about and can tell you all you need to know about your trip. The people are, without doubt, the embodiment of the brand. Their passion for travel and their commitment to customers ultimately delivers the STA Travel brand experience.

Setting up a company that's run by travellers for travellers had other advantages too. STA Travel instinctively knows precisely what its customers want. So not only are its tickets great value – thanks to exclusive contracts negotiated with the airlines – but they are flexible as well, allowing changes to dates of travel or routes.

Over the past three decades, the company has grown exponentially to become a truly global brand. There are over 450 STA Travel branches and a further 1,500 agents

and partners in 85 countries across the world, not to mention a multi-award winning website at www.statravel.co.uk, which now gets more than 400,000 visitors a month in the UK alone. All this, together with an ever expanding product range, from tours to hotels to travel insurance and, yes, now even package holidays, has allowed STA Travel's consultants to provide a better all-round, tailor-made service for their customers.

Yet, despite its success, the company has never lost sight of its core beliefs. The STA Travel brand may have been refined since those early days in Oz, but it remains true to its founders' ideals – fresh, funky, intrepid and innovative. This attitude to life and travel is neatly encapsulated in ad campaigns, promotions, retail design and STA Travel's latest publication, Experience is Everything. This refers not just to the experience of the staff, but also the customers' own on-the-road experiences – experiences that are enlightening, inspiring and form an essential part of travelling. Experiences that continue to make STA Travel the company of choice for over six million people.

And throughout, STA Travel has remained loyal to its core market, which now encompasses all young travellers (and the young at heart) who ascribe to the STA Travel ethos. Ad campaigns at cinemas and music festivals and promotions with other youth brands such as Diesel, HMV, Levi's and Budweiser emphasise STA Travel's place at the very heart of the student and youth market. And just as it remains true to its market, so its customers remain loyal to STA Travel, appreciative of the individual service and the ideals and beliefs that the company represents.

statravel.co.uk

The Lager of Supreme Quality and Worth

Stella Artois is one of the world's best-selling beers and is enjoyed in more than 80 countries. Brewed with traditionally malted barley (germinated on malting floors) and the finest hops, it is renowned for its quality and full flavour.

Few brands can trace their history back as far as 1366, when the Den Horen brewery was first recorded. Sebastian Artois was appointed master brewer in 1708 and bought the brewery in 1717, changing its name to the Artois Brewery.

Stella Artois was first produced as a limited edition Christmas beer, hence the name Stella Artois, after the Christmas Star. It was so popular it became a permanent line. Today, the Stella Artois cartouche still contains the Horn symbol of the original brewery in Belgium and the Christmas Star.

Stella Artois was first imported to the UK in bottles in 1926. Draught Stella Artois was introduced in 1971 and was one of the few premium lagers available in the UK at a time when ales were the dominant drink and standard lagers had a predominately female audience.

In 2002, the Stella Artois Draught Barrel was launched, breaking all beer rules by allowing consumers to consume draught quality beer that stays fresh for up to 28 days after opening at home. Stella Artois is committed to innovations that genuinely enhance the beer drinking experience such as the Draught Barrel, glassware and the new 284ml bottle.

Stella Artois' advertising has always been a key influencer in the successful continuation of the positive brand image. It is famous for breaking the mould of beer advertising, with its up-market style, tone, content and placement, setting Stella Artois apart from its beer rivals. In 1982, Stella Artois introduced the 'Reassuringly Expensive' end-line as the evocative expression of its quality and worth. This was the genesis of its now iconic TV advertising campaign which shows how those who appreciate quality lager would sacrifice anything for a Stella Artois.

What makes these advertisements so memorable are their cinematic scripts and high production values – reflective more of a short film than a beer ad. In fact, ongoing partnerships with notable directors and actors have led to hundreds of creative awards for the brand.

Creativity in advertising has been accompanied by Stella Artois' long-standing association with film (details of current events can be found at stellascreen.co.uk). The

Stella Artois Screen Tour (now in its sixth year) sees the combination of outdoor events (Brighton Beach and Greenwich Park) with more tailored indoor events, combining a classic film in a unique location. Past highlights, such as the screening of Braveheart at Stirling Castle and American Werewolf in London in the disused Aldwych tube station, are remembered by film fans across the UK.

Stella Artois' commitment to film continues on both the big and small screens. Its Channel 4 film sponsorship has been one of the longest standing partnerships on-air, having started in 1997, while Stella Artois Screen's Premiere Club gives registered website users the chance to see a private screening of a cinema release film before its premiere.

Constantly adapting to the challenge of being a leading brand, the future of Stella Artois looks to be just as stand apart as its historic growth. 2004 saw the launch of the After Dark Tour, an eclectic evening inspired by future cinema, bringing together cutting edge film, music and art to deliver a unique multi-media experience. The launch of a new 284ml bottle will continue to see Stella Artois setting trends well into the future.

stellaartois.co.uk

STOLICHNAYA®
GENUINE RUSSIAN VODKA

The authentic Russian vodka

If you read any Russian literature, such as classics by Anton Chekhov, you'll find stories littered with references to drinking. In fact, someone once said that drinking is more important for a Russian than eating, and that's probably true – they do take their drinking seriously, no more so than when it comes to the national drink, vodka.

Stolichnaya is the most famous of all Russian vodkas – a classic spirit that's been produced for over 100 years. It is made to the highest standards, and its superior taste is due to its unique production methods – made from the best winter wheat and pure glacial water, the base spirit is double distilled, then triple filtered.

Stolichnaya originates from a small town in the depths of the Siberian Region of Russia. The town – Irkutusk – is located on the shores of Lake Baikal, one of the greatest wonders of the natural world.

It's now the best selling vodka in the world – and in Russia, a staggering 53 million cases a year are sold. In the UK, it's increasingly popular, having started from humble beginnings. In the late 1980s, while the brand had a vague awareness here through being the vodka of choice for 007 in the earliest (and, it has to be said, the coolest) Bond movies, it was really only found in obscure off-licences. Things started to change, though, when top British barmen and bar owners came across the brand whilst working in the States, where they were so impressed with Stoli's quality, they brought it back to the UK, to use in their bars.

These early aficionados used the Stolichnaya range in their cocktails – as well as serving up straight shots of Stoli over ice. To this day, leading mixologists still use Stolichnaya in their classic vodka concoctions.

Stolichnaya's distinctive label captures the brand's authentic Russian roots, with its Soviet-style, minimalist, logo, featuring the famous 'Moskova' hotel in Moscow. However, the newest addition to the Stoli range, Stolichnaya 'Elit', is presented in a striking new bottle, reflecting the ultra-premium quality of this very special vodka.

Stolichnaya Elit (40% ABV) is only made from the finest fraction of alcohol that runs from the vodka stills, which is then exposed to a unique patented 'freezing' filtration process which no other vodka uses. This is one of the most gentle and effective methods of removing impurities from the vodka, and actually originated centuries ago, from when Russian court distillers would place vodka barrels outside during intensely cold weather. The impurities would then freeze onto the sides of the barrel, and the vodka which remained unfrozen, the smoothest and purest vodka, was then used for the Tsars.

Stoli's reputation means that leading names from the world of fashion and design are happy to be associated with the brand. Elit's UK launch saw some of the world's most renowned designers – including Dolce & Gabbana and Stella McCartney – link with this authentic brand for one of the most stylish and exclusive parties of the year.

The range: Stolichnaya Red (40%), Stolichnaya Blue (50%), Stoli Razberi (37.5%), Stoli Strasberi (37.5%), Stoli Ohranj (37.5%), Stoli Vanil (37.5%). Stolichnaya Gold (40%) and Elit (40%) are available in selected outlets across the UK.

storm®

SOPHIE AS BARDOT

'MY GRANDMOTHER AND MOTHER ARE EXTRAORDINARY LOOKING AND HAVE AMAZING STYLE. THERE ARE FEW PEOPLE AROUND NOW WITH THAT SORT OF GLAMOUR'

PHOTOGRAPHY BY JOSHUA JORDAN

PHOTOGRAPHY BY NICK KNIGHT

PHOTOGRAPHY BY ELLEN VON UNWERTH

PHOTOGRAPHY BY CRAIG MCDEAN

Pioneering the individual

In the seventeen years since Sarah Doukas founded Storm with backing from Virgin, the fashion industry has globalised beyond recognition – and so have the profiles of its leading players. Modelling is one constituent part, and Storm has consistently strived to set new standards for the industry. This can be measured in terms of the achievements of its models and the evolution of the brand.

Two main initiatives characterised Storm's early strategy. The first was to find and develop 'New Faces'. The second was to develop further the careers of the top models, who were gaining international awareness as the faces of designer brands worldwide.

One story encapsulates both these trends, which together have dominated the model industry ever since. It is well documented that Sarah spotted Kate Moss in 1988 at New York's JFK airport, when Kate was fourteen. Four years later, Kate was contracted to Calvin Klein for a worldwide exclusive campaign, an early landmark in a career which has set standards to which all other models aspire. Kate's achievements in the industry are legendary: but it is the consistently superlative quality of her work that sets her apart in the field.

Storm continues to search for the brightest new talent both at home and abroad, and to this end founded sister agency Storm South Africa in 1997. It is now the biggest agency in this burgeoning market, with offices in both Cape Town and Johannesburg.

Storm's philosophy for all of its models is to enable them to attain the highest levels possible. In a competitive environment where individuality and excellence are prized, the most successful models are those who offer something extra: Sophie Dahl, Elle Macpherson,

Eva Herzigova, Carmen Kass and Liberty Ross are rightly acknowledged as stars whose talents reach well beyond the camera lens.

Celebrity culture and media interest have brought modelling into the entertainment world. Recognising this, and in order to allow its brightest talents to develop still further, Storm Artists Management was founded in 1998. Run by top agent Sam Richards, it now represents Oscar winning composers and major actors as well as selected Storm modelling 'alumni' who have successfully moved into other areas.

Taking this idea yet further, in 2003 Storm teamed up with respected brand agency The Brandworks and launched Storm Brand Consulting. This joint venture specialises in creating and managing celebrity-led brand associations.

In a new departure, and building on its position as a 'bridge brand' between the industry and the world at large, Storm has also added www.intothestorm.com, a digital magazine for new ideas. It functions more as an exciting experimental broadcast than as a mere youth magazine, placing Storm at the heart of grass roots level culture and creativity.

But all these adventures into other areas of business refer back to the heart of what Storm does. Modelling involves young people in the core cultural expression which is fashion; and the models in their turn can become icons of their age, when they have the vision, strategy and stewardship which Storm provides.

It was vision which meant Sarah could see Kate Moss' potential at JFK all those years ago: and today, the vision remains the same. Spotted by Storm in Covent Garden, new face Lily Cole has emerged in 2004 to grab some of fashion's top campaigns including Topshop, Anna Sui, Hermes and Prada, as well as the cover of British Vogue.

PHOTOGRAPHY BY RICHARD BUSH FOR NUMERO MAGAZINE

stormmodels.com

TEAC

Last year TEAC celebrated its 50th Anniversary – and with some style. The brand, long known for producing well-built, reliable and innovative audio and audio-video components is now expanding its aspirations and horizons with a collection of outstanding new products which will further increase TEAC's already strong reputation within the consumer electronics field.

Based in a modern facility in Watford, TEAC UK is a subsidiary of the Tokyo-based TEAC Corporation, a billion-dollar global conglomerate and a world leader in recording technology. It's no exaggeration to say that, around the world, the TEAC name – pronounced 'Tee-Ack' – is synonymous with high-quality, high performance consumer products. Not surprising when you consider that TEAC, which started life as the Tokyo Electro Acoustic Company – has been a

leader in the industry since its earliest reel-to-reel recorders.

Today, TEAC manufactures an entire spectrum of components for both high-fidelity audio systems and digitally enhanced home cinemas. For many audiophiles, the TEAC label is a symbol of pride, one that shows they are serious about audio quality. Industry experts and the media share this enthusiasm for TEAC products, giving them consistently high marks for performance. The overwhelming success of the multi-award winning world-famous Reference Series has, over the past few years, helped TEAC gain an enviable status amongst audiophiles and, latterly, with DVD film fans.

Through the Reference Series TEAC has become famous for marrying style with

outstanding performance and since 1996 the
Reference 500 has been an object of desire.
Later, the Reference 300 hi-fi systems and the
highly acclaimed Reference 350 and Reference
550 audio-visual systems have become the
more sophisticated preference among smaller-
component systems, with the range being
regularly updated with emerging technologies.

TEAC is not slow to embrace innovative
and topical technology and incorporate it into
sleek-looking 'lifestyle' designs. Take the Legacy
range – of which much has already been
written in the UK consumer electronics press.
TEAC Legacy Systems are where information
technology meets high-performance audio-
visual entertainment and elegant styling.

The Legacy 700 system has already won 'Best
Buy' status in What Home Cinema magazine and
What Hi-fi? Sound and Vision were so beguiled
by it that it gained Five Stars, swept the board
as winner in a high-powered 'Super Test' and
capped it all by being chosen as the magazine's
outright Winner of the Product of the Year in
the highly coveted and extremely competitive
Best Home Cinema Package category.

TEAC's progress, from reel-to-reel audio in
the 1950s, through its undoubted dominance
of the mid-priced cassette-deck market during
the 1970s and 1980s and the well earned
recognition of excellence in mini-systems with
the Reference Series, is now reaching a turning
point and moving onwards and upwards.

An exciting DAB tuner was introduced into
the Reference Series last year and 2004 saw
the launch of a portable 'Retro' style DAB Radio
and stylish super-mini system – the MC-DX10
– with flat panel NXT speakers. The size of the
speakers mean they'll easily hide away and by
using the sub-woofer included, you can give the
whole piece of kit a boost for large sound from
such a small system. As for musical specifications,
the MC-DX10 has a CD player that will play
CD-Rs, a built-in FM/AM tuner and auxiliary
socket for MP3s or the TV.

The last 50 years has proved to be a long
period of continuing growth in technological
development and innovative design for TEAC.
And with a product line-up stronger and more
exciting than ever, the next 50 years will surely
be as exciting as the last.

teac.co.uk

Ten years ago, if someone suggested the idea of going to a local boozer to sample its culinary delights, the average foodie might be expected to grimace at the unappealing thought of chicken-in-a-basket or reheated scampi. Today, that has all changed: the explosion of the gastro pub phenomenon proves there is a clear demand for both top-notch cooking and avid drinking in the same, comfortable establishment.

Back in 1991 this was not so clear, and it took a small pub in Clerkenwell called the Eagle, run by David Eyre and Mike Belben, to take a big risk and start serving upmarket, restaurant quality food to their unsuspecting clientele. The concept was fresh and simple, just like their food, and eager customers flocked in droves to try their now legendary steak sandwiches.

In the kitchen, watching, learning and admiring, was a keen young chef called Amanda Pritchett, who in 1992 took the Eagle's formula to another level with her own venture, The Lansdowne. She found a historic pub in Primrose Hill, North London, stripped out the fruit machines, TVs and jukebox and brought in reassuringly solid wood furniture and back-to-basics décor. This unassuming local has now become the gastro pub benchmark, earning lavish praise from food critics, locals and rivals alike. Time Out's eating guide recently remarked "Let's not beat about the bush; The Lansdowne offers some of the finest food served in a London pub".

So what keeps The Lansdowne at the front in a now competitive market? The service is laid-back and friendly, but perfunctory. The venue is welcoming and earthy, but shabby. There is no music or entertainment and you have to get out of your seat to order at the bar. The backbone of The Lansdowne's success has been and always will be

Superb food in a battered, bohemian and quintessentially comfortable environment

BAR SNACKS
MARINATED OLIVES £2
MIXED NUTS & SEEDS £2
BOQUERONES £2
(marinated fresh anchovies)
HOMEMADE ... OLIVE OIL £1
CA... ...IND... £2

the quality of its cooking. Amanda Pritchett's philosophy centred on the absolute importance of fresh, uncluttered food in wholesome proportions. There is a generous, Mediterranean approach to the cooking, combining the highest quality ingredients with an aim to provide good, honest pub food.

Not that it is all about the eating: you are just as welcome at this pub propping up the bar and tanking through their range of draft ales and well-selected wines. The venue is now known locally as a celebrity haunt of sorts, but the humble, unpretentious atmosphere just as quickly dismisses any whiff of exclusivity.

Two years ago, James Knight took the helm in the kitchen as Amanda stepped back to concentrate on running the business. James, along with a dedicated team of talented young chefs, has maintained the kind of standards that made The Lansdowne London's leading gastro pub.

At the weekends, the atmosphere in the bar can verge on the boisterous, whilst weekdays see a calmer yet vibrant and talkative crowd converge to shoot the breeze. Upmarket, affluent professionals mix happily with creative types and entrepreneurs, and you are never too far from the ubiquitous local eccentric. There is an informality that oozes from the place, and at the heart of this is Sandy Marshall, the congenial Ex-Groucho club barman and The Lansdowne general manager, who makes sure that the front-of-house operates slickly and efficiently.

As for the future, The Lansdowne has recently opened its sister pub, The Lord Stanley, off Camden Square, which is similarly committed to delivering simple, satisfying dishes to a new audience of eager punters.

The Lansdowne, with its battered, bohemian chic offering a perfect antidote to the dominant, stuffy and trend-conscious restaurant scene, is now a must-visit destination for any serious food fanatic, and no doubt The Lord Stanley will soon be one as well.

Satirical, topical and socially irreverent

Perhaps the most famous, and famously dysfunctional family in the world celebrates its 15th anniversary this year. With the talent contract renewed for another four seasons, until Season nineteen, The Simpsons is the longest-running comedy series in the history of television.

And The Simpsons is still increasing in popularity. Last year, the number of viewers aged between 18-49 – the key TV viewing demographic – actually increased by 8%. Influential film and TV industry magazine The Hollywood Reporter says, "The Simpsons has become a cultural institution on a global scale." More internet searches are performed for The Simpsons than for any other comedy show. And finally, Homer's most common exclamation – 'D'oh!' – has been added to the Oxford English Dictionary.

Since the launch of the series in 1989, stars of film, TV and music have jostled with business and political leaders to provide voices for cartoon characters. Britain's prime minister, Tony Blair, appeared in one episode, together with Sir Ian McKellen and J.K. Rowling.

While initially attacked for contributing to the decline in family values, viewers quickly realised that these odd-looking, yellow cartoon characters actually had more to say about the realities of family life than any of the saccharine-sweet, cloyingly sentimental TV families who had been paraded as role models before.

The Simpsons first appeared on TV in 1987, as a series of animated short films within US TV series, The Tracey Ullman Show. Creator Matt Groening was soon offered a series by Fox, and the rest is TV history. The Simpsons phenomenal success created the whole genre of adult primetime cartoon shows, including Family Guy and Groening's latest, Futurama.

Initially, licensing deals concentrated on Bart, because he was seen as the character with the most kid appeal. But while the show appeals enormously to kids, it is written for a broad audience, and this gives The Simpsons consumer products programme huge potential. Homer, the permanently befuddled father and Bart are normally the two lead characters from a product merchandising

perspective but the richness of The Simpsons brand allows it to support a vast range of product propositions through licensing.

Just as importantly, Fox manages The Simpsons as if it were an FMCG brand, constantly keeping it updated and exploring new possibilities and never allowing it to become over-exposed.

The show is now broadcast in 70 countries with total viewing figures of 70 million. Homer can now say 'D'oh!' in 20 different languages, including Japanese, Chinese and Albanian. Fox estimates that fans of The Simpsons have spent nearly US$2 billion on merchandise since the show was launched in 1989. There are 500 licensees worldwide, with 100 in the UK alone.

In Britain, Sky has been showing The Simpsons since the beginning, while BBC2 had the rights for terrestrial broadcast: but later this year, Channel 4 takes over from the BBC. The move is expected to increase audiences for the show, and is being celebrated with a new logo featuring on over two million licensed Simpsons products and eleven million promotional packs.

Why does The Simpsons have such power? Simple – Bart, Homer, Marge and their family, friends and enemies are universal figures grappling with universal themes, and viewers see themselves whenever they watch.

thesimpsons.com

MATT GROENING

THE SUNDAY TIMES

In the fast pace of modern living, one truth about the week still resonates: Sunday, for most, is the day of rest. Society changes, life changes, opening hours change and working lives change, but for many the old associations ring true. For many, they've never rung truer. Sunday is a day to recharge, to reflect, to take time to stop and stare.

For all these reasons, The Sunday Times 'is the Sunday papers'; for all these reasons, The Sunday Times is a Sunday ritual that goes deeper than news updates. For all these reasons, 3.4 million people read The Sunday Times every week, and it is indisputably Britain's most successful quality newspaper.

People's lives get busier, people's time gets shorter – and The Sunday Times gets bigger. There are now fourteen sections of The Sunday Times to spread out over the duvet or the lounge floor or the pub table. Is this a paradox? No. As people lead busier lives, The Sunday Times takes on the role of editor, sorting out lifestyle information as well as news and sport.

It's a trusted, iconic brand delivering quality information in a format that fits the mood of the day. Information in Sunday time, at Sunday pace.

Since its creation in 1822, The Sunday Times brand has consistently broken new frontiers in the newspaper market. The 21 editors over the past 182 years have kept the brand fresh, exciting and varied, while maintaining its authority and indispensability. In 1958, The Sunday Times became the first paper to appear regularly in two parts by launching the Review section. In 1962, it became the first British newspaper to launch a colour magazine. Now, 42 years on, it is the most diverse and rich newspaper experience available in the UK, with a broad range of sections satisfying its readers' broad interests.

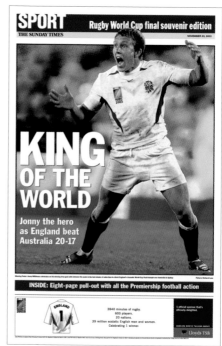

The Business section and The Sunday Times Magazine also continue to set the standard. Business is now Britain's best read publication amongst businessmen: as one reader says, 'On a Monday morning, if you've not read The Sunday Times Business section, you're out of the league of conversations.' The Magazine, similarly, excels, with the strongest identity of any supplement in the market, due to its unparalleled investigative journalism and photography. Both sections continue to win the awards and set the agenda.

Recent initiatives including the groundbreaking launch of the first multimedia newspaper section, The Month, ensure that the brand continues to attract, inspire and influence the younger age group. Designed to deliver the iconic Sunday Times brand in a multimedia environment, The Month has been a huge success, gaining industry awards – 'Best Sales Innovation of the Year 2003' from Campaign magazine – and consumer acclaim.

With agenda-setting content, market-leading innovation and unparalleled breadth and depth, there's little question as to why, for many, The Sunday Times is the Sunday papers.

The Sunday Times now has 1.3 million more readers than its nearest rival, 80% of whom are so committed and loyal that they read no other quality Sunday newspaper. It also now brings in over twice as many 15-34 year olds as its nearest competitor, staying ahead of their ever-growing expectations by continually refreshing content.

The highly successful recent re-launch of the Style section has created an inspirational new home for fashion, providing what readers describe as 'an insider's guide to trends'.

The Sport section continues to lead the pack, with opinion-forming insight and analysis, unique coverage and high impact photography reinforcing its superiority. The highest quality reporters – David Walsh, Hugh McIlvanney – and the best celebrity columnists – including Lawrence Dallaglio and Nick Faldo – consistently indulge readers' sporting passions.

timesonline.co.uk

THE ✦ TIMES

Informs. Absorbs. Entertains. Stimulates.

Founded more than 200 years ago, The Times retains its position as the world's leading newspaper and the paper by which all other papers are judged. It remains at the top of journalistic excellence and newspaper innovation. With more than 1.5 million readers every day in the UK, The Times constantly evolves in response to the needs and desires of its discerning and disparate readership. Informing, absorbing, entertaining and stimulating: The Times chronicles the issues that really matter.

At the forefront of the compact revolution in 2003, The Times demonstrated its progressive personality by deconstructing the polarised 'broadsheet/tabloid' model and recognising that quality writing is not dependent on format. The Times compact demonstrates the paper's commitment to driving change and championing innovation. It has succeeded in bringing new readers to the paper, first attracted by the format and then captivated by the content.

Continuous product development has also led to the creation of new sections, reflecting reader needs and further fuelling their passions. The Game is a weekly section every Monday with every page, every picture, every image, and every word devoted to 'the beautiful game'. Body & Soul is the only section of its kind in the UK newspaper market, a holistic guide to human well-being and potential. Each week, a day before any other paper, Screen has film reviews, industry news and gossip. Reflecting the vibrancy and diversity of the capital, The Knowledge is a weekly insider's guide to life in London. Moreover, The Times boasts T2, the chic and cheeky younger sister of The Times, a magazine every day.

As the definitive dynamic quality newspaper, The Times continues to lead the market in core sections such as news, sport and business, and breaks more news stories than any other newspaper. The paper is turned to for authority, integrity, opinions and perspectives from a vibrant mix of eclectic writers including Julie Burchill, Rod Liddle, Gabby Logan, Robert Crampton, Ginny Dougary, and Caitlin Moran.

As well as outstanding and inventive editorial content, The Times is committed to dynamic design – it now has the most ambitiously designed sections of any newspaper in the world, and has a strength in design, graphics and photography that is unrivalled by any of its competitors.

The Times promotional strategy is to work closely with branding activity to reinforce the values of the product. This includes fostering and developing alliances with appropriate partners. Innovation at The Times extends far beyond the pages: partnerships and promotions touch readers as they live their lives. In 1996, The Times launched the first major sales promotion of any quality newspaper when it joined forces with Eurostar. This partnership is going from strength to strength as it moves into its eighth year. The Times is the principle sponsor of The bfi London Film Festival, establishing itself as the newspaper for film. And The Times is now available exclusively at over 300 Starbucks in the UK, combining coffee and newspapers – two great rituals.

The Times dates back hundreds of years and enjoys the envious status of the UK's most trusted newspaper brand, a highly coveted prize in today's fragmented media landscape. Through its commitment to quality, its vow to innovate and through its ability to connect with its readers, The Times will ensure its longevity and continue to thrive in the 21st century and beyond.

timesonline.co.uk

W

The Wapping Project is housed in the Wapping Hydraulic Power Station, a matchless cultural space on the north bank of the Thames, east of Tower Bridge. Celebrated for its singular combination of challenging contemporary art and performance, fine food and inspiring architecture, it opened to the public in October 2000.

The Wapping Project is the creation of the distinguished theatre director, Jules Wright; its sense of drama is palpable. There is something essentially indefinable about The Wapping Project; it remains an idea in a state of transformation, consistently re-made and re-invented.

The Wapping Hydraulic Power Station was built by the London Hydraulic Power Company in 1890. It harnessed Thames water to provide power to the surrounding docks and throughout the central London area. When it finally closed in 1977, it was the last of its kind in the world.

The conversion of the Wapping Hydraulic Power Station for The Wapping Project was designed and conceived by architectural and design practice SHED 54. Rules were broken to give the contemporary elements a feeling of architectural impermanence – for example, stairs were made from mild steel and deliberately untreated so they would develop a patina of rust.

The brand's visual identity was created by Vince Frost of Frost Design, and is a woodcut especially created to bring together the contemporary and raw elements which signify The Wapping Project. The font was made by taking moulds from the text on the original machinery, and is used on all printed material.

The juxtaposition of the light and transparent qualities of the new with the gravity of the original building intensifies the effect of each. The new architecture identifies with the beauty of the historic building and aims, above all, to create a backdrop against which artists can create audacious contemporary work.

The space also effortlessly incorporates the award-winning restaurant Wapping Food, which spills through the Engine and Turbine Houses. The restaurant is fuelled by the same sense of perfection and ambition, and Wright views the commissioning of the Chefs in much the same way as she does the artists with whom she works. A daily changing menu, in-house butchery and carefully sourced produce have consistently marked out Wapping Food and defined its place within London's most serious restaurants. There are no obvious boundaries between the restaurant and the artistic programme, which is applauded internationally for its quirky, curatorial position.

The body of work produced by The Wapping Project is the product of 20 years' experience and an unchallenged record of commissioning artists who have become major players in the UK's cultural landscape.

All work in the Wapping Hydraulic Power Station is new, commissioned and site-specific. Benchmarks include ALL ABOUT CHAIRS, a series of 33 photography and choreography commissions (July to October 2003); Richard Wilson's extraordinary site-specific work, BUTTERFLY (Spring 2003); NYC, the ground breaking photography show of Magnum photographers and their work on New York (Summer 2002); Elina Brotherus' SPRING photography and video installation (Winter 2001); Solo jazz performances commissioned for JERWOOD: SOLO WITH LIGHT (Winter 2001, later heard on JAZZ ON THREE); Keith Haring's THE TEN COMMANDMENTS (Summer 2001); an extensive choreography series on the external stairwell, STAIRWORKS: JERWOOD:10X8 (Summer 2001); CONDUCTOR by Jane Prophet (Winter 2000), featuring 120 luminescent cables in the flooded Boiler House; and Anya Gallaccio's sublime 34 tonne ice-block, INTENSITIES AND SURFACES commissioned for the derelict building in 1996.

So what is The Wapping Project? It's an idea rooted in a magical building and realised within it. While solid and substantial, it is also mercurial and inexplicable. It's where culture and cool mix.

thewappingproject.com

Tiger Beer, the authentic Far Eastern beer, was introduced into the UK in the 1970s and 1980s by Britain's Chinese community, yearning for their favourite brew from home. But word soon spread outside Chinatowns across the country that Tiger Beer was not just any old Asian beer brand. By the late 1990s, supported by the 'Discover the Tiger' advertising campaign, it had found its way into style bars and trendy pubs as the beer to be seen drinking.

With its sponsorship of events such as underground Thai Kickboxing nights, Asian Extreme Film and Asian Arts, Tiger Beer is inextricably linked with 'Asian Cool' and is well established as a leading player in the niche imported beer segment, offering an exotic and fascinating taste of Asia to UK consumers. And what a taste it is.

Tiger Beer was Singapore's first locally brewed beer, way back in 1932. Created by Asia Pacific Breweries (APB), then known as Malayan Breweries Limited, it owes its distinctive flavour to a particular strain of yeast cultured in Europe especially for APB.

Made from the finest malt barley, yeast and hops, Tiger Beer is now brewed throughout Asia. Some 250 quality control checks are in place to ensure the smooth and consistent flavour which Tiger drinkers have come to expect. It is this consistently high quality and distinctive taste that has won Tiger a string of accolades and awards over the years.

Since its launch, Tiger beer has won no less than 30 gold medals at brewing conventions in cities such as Paris, Rome, Madrid, Lisbon and Geneva. In July 1988, in a blind taste-test involving several hundred brands, the highly

tigerbeer.co.uk

regarded US publication Washingtonian Magazine voted Tiger "Positively the best beer in the world." More recently, Tiger won the Gold Medal at the prestigious 1999 Brewing Industry International Awards, the brewers' equivalent of the Oscars.

Tiger has also inspired literary figures through the decades – it features in the short stories of Somerset Maughan in the 1930s, while in 1946, Anthony Burgess, who would go on to write cult 1960s book A Clockwork Orange, used the brand's then advertising slogan, Time for a Tiger, as the title for a book about life in the mysterious Orient. No wonder Tiger is now the leading beer brand in Singapore and Indo-China, and is enjoyed by beer drinkers from New York to London, Hanoi to Shanghai: in fact, in more than 50 countries across five continents.

In 1998, APB embarked on a global programme to revamp its product packaging design. Tiger's new look is dynamic, distinctive, premium and authentically Far Eastern, with a more contemporary eye-catching logo and distinctive bottle design and print advertising.

In Asia Tiger also supports sports events. It sponsors soccer, such as Singapore's Tiger Beer S-League championships and the Tiger Cup, launched in September 1996 and dubbed the biggest soccer event in Southeast Asia, and was the official beer for the 1997 Southeast Asian Games in Jakarta and the 1997 China National Games in Shanghai.

Tigers, in oriental cultures, are very special animals. The tiger is one of the twelve signs of the Chinese zodiac, and the ancients thought the tiger was one of the noblest animals in existence, with the ability to expel evil and ward off calamities. Up until the early 1900s, tigers used to roam the hundreds of islands which make up the archipelago which now forms modern-day Singapore, Malaysia and Indonesia.

Now, in the 21st century, Tiger beer marries the mystery and history of the Orient with a clean, refreshing taste and a cutting-edge awareness of what's coolest around the world.

TOPSHOP

Topshop has become a retail phenomenon, with a distinctive personality and individual brand mix, hailed in newspapers and fashion magazines for bringing innovation and style to the high street.

Born in 1964 as a department store concession, Topshop grew to become a mediocre high-street store. Mediocre, that was, until it was transformed, under the leadership of brand director Jane Shepherdson, into an achingly modish retailer. Shepherdson – named by Draper's Record as the most influential person on the UK high street – and her team of buyers and designers maintain the brand's leadership by following gut instincts to introduce elements that they feel are right for the brand. This concept is obviously paying dividends, and new Topshop outlets are opening all the time – most recently in High Street Kensington and Birmingham. There are now 285 stores in the UK and a further 63 internationally.

Today, the Oxford Circus flagship is the world's largest fashion store, with 90,000 ft², over 200 changing rooms and 1,000 staff on duty at any one time. It attracts 180,000 visitors each week, including an impressive celebrity

following including the likes of Kate Moss, Gwyneth Paltrow, Erin O'Connor and Elizabeth Jagger. There is also increasing awareness for Topshop abroad – particularly among the jet setters of New York and LA. Indeed, in February 2004, the LA Times wrote: "In today's topsy-turvy fashion world, Topshop's designers create the pieces that style icons such as Moss and Paltrow incorporate into their own eclectic wardrobes."

One key ingredient in the brand's success has been its vision of shopping as entertainment – the Oxford Circus store has its own music channel, Topshop Kitchen, Boutique space that houses designer collections, a dedicated Vintage space as well as a deluxe Nail Bar. There are also frequent in-store events, such as seasonal catwalk shows and fashion and beauty makeovers, all of which offer the Topshop customer a complete and exciting shopping experience. The formula evidently works – visitors to the store spend an average of 44 minutes inside.

Another reason for the brand's success is the constant evolution of Topshop Unique. Unique was created to dispel the myth that Topshop's sole aim was to copy the

catwalk, and to instead establish its reputation as an authority in fashion, constantly pushing the boundaries, appealing to its designer-aware customers, celebrities and industry insiders alike.

Alongside this, the TS Design label features designer collaborations from Sophia Kokosalaki, Jonathan Saunders, Jens Laugesen, Zandra Rhodes and House of Jazz. Other new product initiatives include the launch of 'b', the first maternity collection for Topshop, and the extension of the Style Advisor service with Topshop To Go, a mobile fashion service, where representatives from the Style Advisor team take Topshop collections into the homes and workplaces of customers. August 2004 saw the exciting launch of Topshop's first stand-alone shoe store in Manchester, selling the ultimate fashionable footwear.

Topshop is also the biggest supporter of young fashion designers in the industry, supporting talent at a grass-root level. Annual sponsorship programmes include Graduate Fashion Week and the New Generation London Fashion Week Award, where financial support and a promotional platform is offered to Britain's exciting young fashion talent. Topshop has also won a whole slew of awards from the industry and from magazines and newspapers – Drapers Record, The Face, The Sunday Times, The Independent, Glamour, InStyle, Company… the list goes on.

Finally, there is the brand's website – www.topshop.co.uk – which remains unrivalled as an online fashion destination. With approximately 100 new product lines added to the site a week and around 800 lines on the web at any one time, www.topshop.co.uk has over 120,000 email subscribers. The site has doubled sales year on year and is due to launch a fantastic vintage range this summer.

topshop.co.uk

TRAILFINDERS

THE TRAVEL EXPERTS

> Independent travel for the
> independently minded

For the past 34 years, Trailfinders has been at the cutting edge of all things 'travel', maintaining a reputation for honesty, authenticity and integrity in an ever-changing market. Where rivals are constantly following trends, Trailfinders instead elects to set them.

Former SAS Officer Mike Gooley founded Trailfinders in 1970 with a staff of four as an overland tour company. By 1972, Trailfinders had become the first independent flight consolidator, offering exceptional value airfares worldwide. Bucking the trend for package holidays, Trailfinders also pioneered the concept of tailor-made travel, where each holiday and each client is treated as unique.

In 1989, Trailfinders opened its flagship travel centre in the heart of London – a state-of-the-art 'one-stop travel shop' complete with Travel Clinic, retail space for books and travel essentials, Passport and Visa Service, a dedicated First and Business Class department and a unique Information Centre.

Today, Trailfinders sends in excess of 720,000 clients abroad each year and employs over 1,000 staff across eighteen travel centres in the UK, Ireland and Australia. The Trailfinders Group now includes an airline, sports club, luxury rainforest lodge in Far North Queensland and even a catering company. In addition, the Mike Gooley Trailfinders Charity has donated £10 million in the last five years, mainly to cancer research.

Despite its tremendous growth, the company remains privately owned and continues to be a trusted innovator in the world of travel. From long weekends in New York

to safaris in Africa, beach retreats in Asia to skiing in North America or even dream holidays in Australia, Trailfinders still offers unbeatable value and service.

Trailfinders can boast numerous awards, not just from the trade but, more importantly, from the public – Observer readers voted it Best Travel Agent on five occasions and Telegraph readers awarded it Best Independent Travel Specialist for the last three years.

Word of mouth has always been Trailfinders' strongest marketing tool – over 80% of clients are previous customers or were referred by friends – while the Trailfinder Magazine, published three times a year and reaching over 750,000 households, keeps clients abreast of the latest products and travel ideas.

While Trailfinders does have a website there is a deep-seated belief that there is no substitute for the value of the human touch. The Trailfinders brand is built

around the skill of its travel consultants to piece together complex itineraries while maintaining the highest level of customer service. Call Trailfinders, and the person dealing with your travel arrangements will usually be a graduate who has travelled extensively in at least two continents and has probably been to where you want to go.

Whatever department they subsequently move to, the likelihood is they will have started their careers dealing with the public face to face. As a result, through every level of the company there is an understanding of what the customer wants and how to deliver it. From founder to consultant, the passion for travelling and the sense of enjoyment which stems from working with like-minded people is immediately apparent.

The expectations and aspirations of travellers have evolved since the original backpacker discovered Trailfinders in 1970. As their circumstances have changed, their needs have broadened to include family holidays or the world's most exclusive hotels. In fact, First and Business Class travel is one of the fastest growing areas for the company, representing 20% of annual turnover. Yet the desire for an out-of-the-ordinary experience remains, and Trailfinders continues to be true to its roots, catering for all manner of travellers united by one thing: the desire to experience their chosen destination to the full.

trailfinders.com

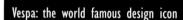
Vespa: the world famous design icon

The Vespa is one of the world's most enduring symbols of cool: yet, when the legend was born in 1946, no-one could have guessed that it would attain such iconic stature, standing the test of time for nearly 60 years.

Manufacturer Enrico Piaggio's humble vision was to meet Italy's urgent need for modern affordable transport. He asked Corradino D'Ascanio, an aeronautical engineer who created the first modern helicopter, to design a simple, robust vehicle for men and women, which would not dirty its rider's clothes and which could also carry a passenger.

The scooter had to be affordable and functional, a vehicle for the masses to get Italy moving again after World War II. Ironically, the very features which made it so practical – the 'step-through' seating position, simple mechanics and metal body – are still fundamental to its personality, and are the foundations upon which the entire scooter industry has been built. Yet no other scooter has ever come close to the Vespa in terms of image, status or appreciation.

The Vespa gained worldwide recognition when Audrey Hepburn and Gregory Peck weaved through the streets of Rome on one in Roman Holiday (1953). After years of austerity, the 1950s saw a new exuberance start to emerge, and the sight of two young lovers astride a Vespa in the capital of romance captured the hearts of millions. When the Vespa was adopted by the English Mods some years later, the thrill had a harder edge, a hint of danger and rebellion.

The classic romance of Roman Holiday and the defiant non-conformity of Mod culture combined with the innate Italian-ness of the Vespa to create the image to which so many still aspire. As Italian author, Umberto Eco, says, "The Vespa came to be linked in my eyes with transgression, sin and temptation."

More than 138 different versions of the Vespa have been produced, and over sixteen million sold since 1946. Whether a classic machine or the latest Vespa Granturismo (launched in 2003), the curve of the body, the angle of the wing mirrors, the shape of the headlight are always inimitably Vespa, while the logo on the front shield is recognised and coveted the world over.

The Vespa logo is itself a design classic and now appears on clothing and accessories, enabling everyone to buy into the Vespa legend. Of course, everything carrying the logo must combine practicality, beauty and quality, with a touch of that indefinable essence of Vespa.

Much of Vespa's marketing is about being in the right place at the right time, being seen with the right people and associating with the right brands in order to reinforce its aspirational image. Such associations include customisations by people such as Salvador Dali, Vivienne Westwood and Dolce & Gabbana; events and exhibitions; appearances in dozens of films; and celebrities through the ages extolling the virtues of the Vespa. The image has always been carefully handled, with each marketing opportunity assessed to ensure that it fits absolutely with the brand.

The Vespa has also featured in many of the most famous museums in the world, including The Guggenheim, The Design Museum and Le Centre Georges Pompidou – testimony to its place in design and automotive history. Indeed, Vespa now has its own museum, in Pontedera, Italy, where the scooter's heritage can be traced through the years.

From its inception 58 years ago, the Vespa has remained true to the original legend and the unique values that consumers buy into – adventure, style and simplicity. The design, although modified, never changes. One look, and you can tell it's a Vespa.

vespa.com

virgin atlantic

Distinctive, fun-loving, innovative and continually offering a higher level of luxury

Launched in 1984, Virgin Atlantic started life as an eccentricity – an unexpected offshoot of Richard Branson's mainly music-based Virgin Group. The ebullient entrepreneur launched the airline in just three months, finding an aircraft, designing uniforms and then setting off on an inaugural flight to New York with a planeload of his friends, celebrities and media.

The giants of the industry didn't rate the cheeky newcomer's chances very highly. Little did they know that, 20 years on, Virgin Atlantic would be Britain's second largest long haul carrier and the third largest European carrier across the North Atlantic.

Customers flocked to the new airline that treated them as individuals and that combined good service and value with style and fun. Everything about its attitude was quintessentially Virgin: the small newcomer taking on the complacent and established giants; the people's champion, offering lower fares and better service whilst maintaining

quality and innovative product developments.

The airline industry was affected more than most by the tragic events of September 11th 2001. There was an immediate and significant reduction in passengers, and a number of airlines suffered bankruptcy. Passenger confidence is slowly rebuilding but it will be some time before the long-term consequences are fully apparent. It is clear, though, that to compete in this challenging environment, it is vital for airlines to adapt and evolve an ever-improving range of services.

Even though it has now grown up, Virgin Atlantic still retains a sense of style which sets it apart from its rivals. Its Upper Class service has set new standards of comfort and innovation and the award-winning Upper Class Suite, launched in 2003, has taken the promise of a first class product for a business class fare to new heights. It consists of a reclining leather seat for take off, a place to sit and eat a

proper meal opposite your partner, the longest fully flat bed on any airliner in the world with a proper mattress for sleeping on, a private on-board bar to drink at with your friends, a private massage room and four limousines per return trip – all at a price thousands of pounds less than other airline's First Class. It has already proved to be a massive success, winning the airline all-important market share along with an impressive array of awards.

The same goes for economy and premium economy, which also challenge the norms of air travel, with levels of comfort and service not offered by other airlines. On-board entertainment has always been Virgin Atlantic's forte. It was the first airline to offer business class passengers individual TVs, back in 1989, and the first to provide personal TV screens offering a choice of channels to passengers in all classes, in 1991. Virgin Atlantic continues to push the boundaries of in-flight entertainment technology, offering passengers over 200 hours of video and audio on demand, SMS text messages and email and many computer games.

The greatest and best known advertisement for Virgin is Richard Branson himself. Often perceived as the 'consumer hero', Virgin's brand values reflect his own personality. At one and the same time Branson is one of the UK's most admired businessmen, and one of the most flamboyant. His daredevil antics, such as ballooning across the Atlantic, have given Virgin extra publicity.

The airline's TV advertisements, featuring icons like Helen Mirren, Anna Friel, Iggy Pop and even Miss Piggy, accentuate the message that Virgin Atlantic is anything but 'just another airline'. Like these brand ambassadors, Virgin Atlantic owes its success to challenging the status quo, dictating rather than following fashion, and constantly reinventing its image to stay fresh in consumers' minds.

virgin.com/atlantic

V V Rouleaux

V V Rouleaux's ribbons and trimmings shops have been called by some in the fashion and design worlds "the perfect antidote to minimalism": to others, they are "sex on a spool." Either way, there is general agreement that they stick "two fingers up at everything that is boring and staid."

Yet back in 1990, when Annabel Lewis closed down her flower shop in Fulham and transformed it into a ribbon shop, she was taking a brave leap. Traditional haberdashery shops were largely a thing of the past, and customers looking for ribbons and bows found themselves searching small areas in aging department stores where tired displays did nothing for the products on offer.

Annabel, however, was certain that it was not the demand for ribbons that had fallen, but the quality and variety of the products on offer. She thought that if you sourced the best products from around the world, and

> Ribbons are no longer just for Christmas — they're for life

displayed them to their best advantage, then discerning buyers would beat a path to your door. And she was right.

Within three years, the shop had moved to Sloane Square and this outlet would be joined by another in Marylebone High Street and the Trade Vaults in Battersea. As The Times would later write, "millions of metres and many devoted customers later, the rest is fashion history", as well as describing it as 'a brilliant concept'.

Annabel's secret is simple — in theory, at least. She sources from all over the world; rather than going through wholesalers, she deals directly with the manufacturers; and she begs them to continue making intricate and beautiful products by traditional manufacturing processes. She quickly discovered types and styles of ribbons never seen in this country before, from Japanese organdy to French wire-edged tafettas.

By promoting skill, knowledge and experience over mass production, she creates a freshness which makes shopping at V V Rouleaux a sublime experience. Annabel's knowledge and no-nonsense enthusiasm have created new markets and brought in new customers. Where else can you find African necklaces as tie-backs, chandelier crystals as curtains, leather corsages, feather butterflies – and over 50 colours of satin ribbon in seven widths?

Whilst the V V Rouleaux retail outlets provide the high street with the solution to every fashion and decorating dilemma, the trade side has inspired a whole generation of textile, interior, and fashion designers. Gold braid, hand painted flowers, beaded fringes, butterflies and suede ribbons are despatched to restaurants, film sets, fashion chains, and exclusive shops all over the world. Customers now range from PR and advertising companies to fashion designers and interior decorators, from craft shops to large retailers.

V V Rouleaux further developed its offering with its Atelier range of furniture and other products with a passementerie theme, whether contemporary or traditional. Many of the ideas and designs come from the company's archive collection of ribbons and trimmings. Chairs and sofas are deep-buttoned, covered in antique millinery velvet, and trimmed with ribbons dating from the early part of the last century. Cushions and lampshades are covered with beads and raffia, handbags in felt, and slippers delicately embroidered.

V V Rouleaux has grown from a niche shop in Fulham to the most creative ribbons and trimmings company in Europe with its own retail shops, trade vaults and design offices. It has become the ultimate destination for anyone interested in fashion or interior design, or as House & Garden magazine says, for anyone "spurred on by the thrill of discovering something unique. For here is indeed something for everyone."

vvrouleaux.com

Wallpaper*

From seating systems to swimming trunks, hotel lobbies to television screens, Wallpaper* is the magazine that celebrates design. Launched in 1996, Wallpaper* instantly became the international style bible with its unique coverage of interiors, architecture, entertainment, fashion and travel. Eight years later, it continues to be the ultimate arbiter of style and design.

From the outset, Wallpaper* redefined cool for successful, design-conscious professionals. These young but cash-rich men and women wanted a new combination of exclusivity, luxury and contemporary design. And now they could discover a world of sophisticated travel, boutique hotels and cutting-edge restaurants, courtesy of Wallpaper*. A new lifestyle was born, where luxury was core and taste a given.

Access to the best the world has to offer

Now under the direction of editor-in-chief Jeremy Langmead, the magazine is the only international luxury design and lifestyle magazine in the world, and sold in no less than 50 countries. When Langmead joined the team at the end of 2002 he instigated a major shift in attitude that saw the magazine move away from its minimalist Scandinavian look to one which is much more eclectic. Along with the new Creative Director, Tony Chambers, Langmead was responsible for the June 2003 redesign, which gave the magazine a more modern but elegant, sophisticated and sexy look that espoused Wallpaper's core philosophy of intelligent luxury. The industry reacted positively to the changes, with favourable comments in the international press – for example, Melissa Pordy said in the New York Times, "Wallpaper is a magazine that reaches the forecasters of style and design… a unique ability to deliver an influential audience."

In 2004 the Wallpaper* brand has been extended to include a new biannual city guide, Navigator*, and internet site, wallpaper.com. Each Navigator* selects ten cities that will form the essential destination hit list for the affluent cosmopolitan traveller; the first two issues ranged from London to Ljubljana, Milan to Mumbai with tailor-made itineraries to inspire weekend jaunts and inject designer living into repetitive business trips. Already, Navigator* has become the perfect accessory for the design-conscious, time-restricted, luxury-loving, info-hungry traveller.

Wallpaper.com has been launched to satisfy the demand of people wanting quick access to Wallpaper's current and historic content. With over half a million unique users in its first month, the site is sure to be a winner for regular readers and design-savvy web users.

With its ever-growing pool of talent – photographers such as Tobias Madörin and writers such as Hari Kunzru – Wallpaper* is consolidating its position as the international authority on luxury living. Its network of international contributors based in the world's major cities constantly seek out new nuggets of information, objects of desire and places to deliver the magazine's new promise: "Access to the best the world has to offer."

wallpaper.com

Weber. Born in Chicago.

The Weber barbecue has been the signature shape of barbecues for more than five decades. Undeniably American – uncompromising and functional – it created a culture of outdoor cooking almost single-handed, and has become as essential to the American way of life as the pick-up truck and the tail-gate party.

It's the realisation of a company true to its core values, whose belief in its products came long before it knew it had found acceptance, and before it realised it had created a brand known as Weber.

It's one man's vision; and yet it doesn't even bear his name. In 1952, George Stephen built a better barbecue for himself. Irritated by the unappetising food the barbecues of the day produced, he just made one of his own. George did not set out to create a brand – just a better barbecue.

George worked for Weber Brothers Metal Works in Chicago, a small metal bending company specialising in parts for other products. From a large metal sphere, bent for harbour buoys used on Lake Michigan, George fashioned the first kettle-shaped barbecue. Instinctively, he knew a rounded cooking bowl with a lid was the key to success. Adding three legs for stability, a lid handle and special vents, he took the strange looking object home.

Friends and neighbours laughed at first – but quickly changed their opinion after tasting George's food. Reluctantly, he started making the kettles for friends; soon, George's 'folly' was in such hot demand he could not make them fast enough.

More than 50 years have passed since that first Weber kettle, but its lineage can be traced right through to the ones made today. The fundamentals are unchanged, while any refinements are a testament to a company philosophy of building only the highest quality products, and to a desire for constant improvement.

Every Weber grill comes with that same legacy of caring built in — perfectionist dedication to building the best grill you can buy. Weber knows the last thing you want to contend with is poor construction and burnt food with friends and family around.

George Stephen's legacy is evident today, through the twelve children he raised, and who now carry on his work at Weber. Maybe that's why there's a Weber difference which people have responded to in such positive and passionate ways. They appreciate that the Weber badge stands for something tangible and relevant. It stands for exceptional products that produce exceptional results. It stands for the pride and confidence to stand behind our products — now, and for their working life. It also stands for the distinctive taste that comes from food prepared on a Weber grill.

Now, there's a Weber for everyone, portable grills to luxury gas cooking systems. Weber's imaginative, thoughtful design is the constant, delivering exceptional construction, and practical convenience.

And you can trust a brand that stands behind its products. Its job does not end with the sale: Weber owners expect the very best and the brand delivers, with a warranty programme that you would expect from the world's leading brand of barbecues.

Free time is now a very precious commodity and every conceivable modern-day distraction is available. Strange, therefore, that more and more families and friends are returning, time and again to that same simple pleasure that George was so passionate about. It's more than cooking. It's more than eating. It's connecting with friends, with family. It's the embodiment of all these things that can be found only in a Weber.

Thank you, George.

weber.com

It's good to play together

If you love video games, then you will love Xbox. The world's most powerful games console continues to go from strength to strength, with an incredible cutting edge online service, some of the best games on the market, superlative graphics and awesome audio output leaving even its closest rivals in its wake.

Xbox was launched in 2001 with a mission to be the most powerful video game experience available. The launch was hailed by many as the greatest ever, with over 1.5 million consoles being sold worldwide by December that year. Since then, Xbox has established itself as one of the most popular consoles on the market and looks set to sell over sixteen million consoles worldwide by 2004.

Setting it apart from its rivals is the revolutionary online games service, Xbox Live. Launched in March 2003, the service enables gamers to play games and speak to one another in real-time, wherever they are in the world. Xbox Live is currently host to nearly one million gamers across the globe in 24 countries. Games such as Project Gotham Racing 2, Rainbow Six 3, Counter-Strike and Top Spin head an impressive list of titles that keeps gamers across the

globe glued to their sofa for hours. The portfolio of Live-enabled games – which looks set to reach 150 by the end of 2004 – will be bolstered by a recent announcement that Electronic Arts will develop a number of their top sports titles for the service, including FIFA 2005.

Following the success of a limited edition translucent-green console launched in 2003, Xbox bettered it in 2004 with a limited edition crystal console which rapidly became a collector's item and style icon for gamers.

This year, Xbox announced a partnership with the McKenzie Group to install Xbox Play Zone networks in Carling Academy venues across the UK. This followed previous deals which have seen Xbox become the games console of choice for Powerleague five-a-side venues and Scream Bars across the UK.

Xbox also trumpeted the sponsorship of BaySixty6, the newly revamped London Skate Park. After speaking to local skaters to see what they wanted in the venue, Xbox built a host of new ramps and jumps and created a gaming zone before re-opening it as London's premier skate venue.

And it's not just at home in the UK that Xbox has been entertaining the masses…

March 2004 saw the console head to the slopes for 'Xbox Big Day Out'. The event is one of Europe's biggest freestyle ski and snowboard events and saw over 100,000 spectators descend upon Val D'Isere. And in July Xbox was back in Ibiza to entertain the masses for the annual 'We Love Xbox' night at Space.

But that's all in the past – how about the future?

On November 9th 2004, the world's most highly anticipated game sequel will be released exclusively on Xbox – Halo 2. The original Halo is hailed by many as the greatest console game ever produced and has sold over four million copies worldwide.

More than 300 games are now available for Xbox and the future looks set to be even more exciting with titles such as Doom 3, Fable, Forza Motorsport, and Jade Empire all illustrating Microsoft's commitment to offering cutting-edge games on Xbox.

So whether you're a serious die-hard games enthusiast or more of a social gamer, Xbox is fast becoming the console of choice across the globe.

xbox.com/uk

Agent Provcateur
Agent Provocateur Ltd
18 Mansfield Street
London
W1G 9NW

Asahi
Asahi Beer Europe Ltd
17 Connaught Place
London
W2 2EL

Audi
Audi UK
Yeomans Drive
Blakelands
Milton Keynes
MK14 5AN

Barbican
Barbican Centre
Silk Street
London
EC2Y 8DS

BlackBerry®
BlackBerry/Research In Motion
Centrum House
36 Station Road
Egham
Surrey
TW20 9LF

Bose
Bose UK Ltd
1 Ambley Green
Gillingham Business Park
Gillingham
Kent
ME8 0NJ

British Airways London Eye
British Airways London Eye
Riverside Building
County Hall
Westminster Bridge Road
London
SE1 7PB

Budweiser Budvar
Budweiser Budvar UK Ltd
Hamilton House
Mableon Place
London
WC1H 9BB

Campari
Gruppo Campari
Via Turati, 27
20121 Milan (MI)
Italy

Chanel
Chanel Ltd
19-21 Old Bond Street
London
W1S 4PX

Coca-Cola
Coca-Cola Great Britain
1 Queen Caroline Street
Hammersmith
London
W6 9HQ

Coutts
Coutts & Co
440 Strand
London
WC2R OQS

Dazed & Confused
Dazed & Confused
112-116 Old Street
London
EC1V 9BG

Denon
Denon UK
Chiltern Hill
Chalfont St Peter
Bucks
SL9 9UG

Dermalogica
Dermalogica
Caxton House
Randalls Way
Leatherhead
Surrey
KT22 7TW

Design Museum
Design Museum
Shad Thames
London
SE1 2YD

Diesel
Diesel London Ltd
55 Argyle Street
London
WC1H 8EE

Diet Coke
Coca-Cola Great Britain
1 Queen Caroline Street
Hammersmith
London
W6 9HQ

Dust
Dust
27 Clerkenwell Road
London
EC1M 5RN

GAGGIA
Gaggia UK Ltd
Crown House
Mile Cross Road
Halifax
HX1 4HN

**Goldsmiths College,
University of London**
Goldsmiths College,
University of London
New Cross
London
SE14 6NW

Guinness
Diageo plc
Lakeside Drive
Park Royal
London
NW10 7HQ

Hakkasan
Hakkasan Ltd
6th Floor
16-19 Gresse Street
London
W1T 1QL

Havana Club
Pernod Ricard UK
Central House
3 Lampton Road
Middlesex
Hounslow
TW3 1HY

innocent
innocent Ltd
Fruit Towers
3 Goldhawk Estate
Brackenbury Road
London
W6 0BA

Land Rover
Land Rover
Banbury Road
Gaydon
Warwickshire
CV35 0RR

L'Artisan Parfumeur
L'Artisan Parfumeur
14-16 Regent Street
London
SW1Y 4PH

Lavazza
Lavazza Coffee (UK) Ltd
4-6 Silver Road
White City
London
W12 7SG

Linn
Linn Products Ltd
Glasgow Road
Waterfoot
Eaglesham
Glasgow
G76 0EQ

Malmaison
Malmaison Brand Ltd
1 West Garden Place
Kendal Street
London
W2 2AQ

MTV
MTV Networks UK & Ireland
17-29 Hawley Crescent
London
NW1 8TT

Nokia
Nokia Mobile Phones
(UK) Sales Ltd
Headland House
The Chord Business Park
London Road
Godmanchester
PE29 2NX

O₂
O₂ UK Ltd
260 Bath Road
Slough
Berkshire
SL1 4DX

Orange
Orange Personal
Communications Services Ltd
St James Court
Great Park Road
Almondsbury Park
Bradley Stoke
Bristol
BS32 4QJ

PUMA
Puma United Kingdom Ltd
Challenge Court
Barnett Wood Lane
Leatherhead
Surrey
KT22 7LW

Richard James
Richard James
29 Savile Row
London
W1S 2EY

Rizla
Rizla
UK Division
PO Box 525
Southville
BS99 1LQ

Ruby & Millie
The Boots Company plc
Buidling D98
Thane Road
Nottingham
NG90 2JF

Saab
Saab Great Britain Ltd
150 Bath Road
Maidenhead
Berks
SL6 4LB

sass & bide
Magnolia PR
Studio 211
Westbourne Studios
242 Acklam Road
London
W10 5JJ

Selfridges
Selfridges & Co
400 Oxford Street
London
W1A 1AB

Somerset House
Somerset House Trust
South Building
Somerset House
Strand
London
WC2R 1LA

Sony Ericsson
Sony Ericsson Mobile
Communications
1 Lakeside Road
Aerospace Centre
Farnborough
GU14 6XP

Sophia Kokosalaki
Untitled Management Ltd
7-10 Charlottte Mews
London
W1T 4EE

STA Travel
STA Travel
Priory House
6 Wrights Lane
Hammersmith
London
W8 6TA

Stella Artois
Interbrew UK Ltd
Porter Tun House
500 Capability Green
Luton
Bedfordshire
LU1 3LS

Stolichnaya
First Drinks Brands Ltd
Imperial House
Imperial Way
Southampton
Hampshire
SO15 0RB

Storm Model Management
Storm Model Management Ltd
5 Jubilee Place
London
SW3 3TD

TEAC
TEAC UK Ltd
5 Marlin House
Marlins Meadow
Watford
Hertfordshire
WD18 8TE

The Lansdowne
The Lansdowne
90 Gloucester Avenue
Primrose Hill
London
NW1 8HX

The Simpsons
Twentieth Century Fox
Film Co Ltd
31/32 Soho Square
London
W1D 3AP

The Sunday Times
Times Newspapers Ltd
1 Virginia Street
London
E98 1GE

The Times
Times Newspapers Ltd
1 Virginia Street
London
E98 1GE

The Wapping Project
The Wapping Project
Wapping Hydraulic
Power Station
Wapping Wall
London
E1W 3ST

Tiger Beer
Tiger Export (UK)
4th Floor
Hamilton House
Mabledon Place
London
WC1H 9BB

Topshop
Arcadia Group Ltd
Colegrave House
70 Berners Street
London
W1T 3NL

Trailfinders
Trailfinders Ltd
9 Abingdon Road
London
W8 6AH

Vespa
Piaggio Ltd
1 Boundary Row
London
SE1 8HP

Virgin Atlantic
Virgin Atlantic Airways
The Office
Crawley Business Quarter
Manor Royal
Crawley
West Sussex
RH10 9NU

V V Rouleaux
V V Rouleaux
Head Office
6 Tun Yard
Peardon Street
London
SW8 3HT

Wallpaper*
Wallpaper*
Brettenham House
Ground Floor
Lancaster Place
London
WC2E 7TL

Weber
Weber Stephen Products
(UK) Ltd
High Laithe
Gargrave Road
Broughton
Skipton
North Yorkshire
BD23 3AW

Xbox
Microsoft Ltd
Thames Valley Park
Reading
Berkshire
RG6 1WG